CORNERSTONE

GUIDELINES FOR RELIGIOUS EDUCATION

I.

CORNERSTONE

by

Kevin Nichols

Commissioned by and published with the authority of
The Bishops' Conference of England and Wales

St Paul Publications

St Paul Publications
Middlegreen, Slough SL3 6BT

Copyright © St Paul Publications
First published November 1978
Printed in Great Britain by the Society of St Paul, Slough
ISBN 0 85439 157 6

Contents

Foreword

The subject of catechetics and religious education in recent years has produced sometimes more heat than light. Extreme opinions have been asserted with vigour. Some seemed to be saying that everything done in the past was wrong, others that nothing done in the present was right. Extremes indeed but opinions felt and, therefore, deserving careful consideration.

The time is ripe for an assessment of the current thinking on the subject over the whole field of the Church's apostolate. For religious education is not confined within the school: indeed, the last Roman Synod of Bishops put adult education in the forefront.

Monsignor Kevin Nichols is National Adviser for Religious Education appointed by the Bishops' Conference. Before that he taught in Christ's College, Liverpool. He is, therefore, well qualified to give guidance on the subject.

This book, *Cornerstone,* is the first in a projected series of nine under the general title of 'Guidelines'.

Cornerstone offers the basic theory of religious education but has sufficient examples of practical application to make it not simply 'theoretical'. Monsignor Nichols takes into account modern teaching practice and theory and at the same time specifically Catholic experience and Catholic reflection on the philosophy and theology of education. The documents of Vatican II and the General Catechetical Directory and the Liturgical and other Instructions of the Holy See are always at his elbow.

He faces squarely the question of teaching with authority, 'submission to a word spoken from beyond ourselves' (§ 84), and the charge of 'indoctrination' (§ 17). On this he is balanced and judicious as on many other matters of debate today, for example on the question of the expression of the Faith in Propositions (§ 216 and ff).

He argues cogently for a revival of Apologetics whilst taking account of the changed and changing situation both educational and cultural.

He has wise words on the need to link catechetics with life as it is lived so that religion is not regarded as 'essentially an intellectual and sophisticated thing': "It belongs also to the little ones, the handicapped and the failures and those who cannot cope with the problems of life," who all 'have a role in the Church not just as objects of pastoral compassion' (§ 115).

There is much wisdom, humanity and experience in these pages and a serene eirenical temper when speaking of other than the Catholic experience.

Monsignor Nichols undertook his task at the request of the Bishops' Conference. I thank him warmly on its behalf and I am glad to commend this first instalment of 'Guidelines' which is now published with the authority of the Conference.

+ GEORGE PATRICK DWYER
President
Bishops' Conference of England and Wales.

"This is the stone that was rejected by the builders but which has become the head of the corner".

(Acts 4:11)

"For when we in our human frailty have some task to perform, for instance when we are building a house, we begin the work by preparing our materials and after this beginning we dig deeply. Next we put stones into this foundation and then we place walls upon it in rising courses of stones and so, litttle by little, we reach completion in accomplishing the task upon which we have set out".

(Bede: *Commentary on Genesis* I ii 8-14)

SECTION I

CLEARING THE GROUND

Chapter 1

Words and Meanings

1.   Catholics argue a great deal among themselves and in the papers about religious education. These arguments are painful to those who love their faith and are used to presenting a united front to the world. Nevertheless, times of rapid change call for a reassessment of our pastoral and educational work. Many different facts about the faith and about the modern world have to be borne in mind. We have to be like the wise man in the gospel who is praised for "taking out of his treasure-house things new and old". Differences of opinion are bound to arise. Heated arguments hurt. But they are a tribute to the anxious concern felt by parents, priests and teachers for the future of our children. Yet there comes a time when the arguing has to stop. We must act and we must act together. This means agreeing on principles. It means being prepared to carry out the policy which follows from them. Our faith does leave room for differences of opinion about what should be done. But faith is not in itself a matter of opinion. We hold it as members of the Body of Christ. When important questions concerning its life and work arise, that Body must act in unison. It is the duty of the bishops of the Church to make sure that the unity and truth of the faith is preserved; and that the teaching of the faith is realised in practicable and effective policies.

2.   Some people think that arguments arise only because people use the same words with different meanings. If we all made it clear what exactly we mean by the words we use, differences of opinion would disappear. This is a mistaken view. There are important differences of belief independent of the words that express them. Nevertheless many problems can be cleared up if words are more clearly defined. How often do arguments begin with, "It all depends what you mean by . . ."? We are going to begin by trying to say clearly what we mean by four words which

are often used in connection with religious education. Two of them are especially important for they are often used as though they were interchangeable although their meaning is in fact considerably different.

These are the words "catechesis" and "religious education" itself. The other pair which are less confusing we shall deal with first. They are "religious studies" and "evangelisation".

3.   By this is meant quite simply, the objective study of religion as we find it in history and in the world of today. It makes no assumptions about the belief of either teacher or learner. It can be done, at least in theory, equally well by Christians, Buddhists, agnostics or atheists. Nor does it try to influence anyone towards belief either generally or specifically. It simply deals in external facts, information about and understanding of the variety of religious life and the different aspects of it. It has this serious limitation.

A purely external view can lead us to misunderstand reality; just as an external view of our fellow-men can lead us to judge their real human quality quite wrongly. Nonetheless it is useful, especially nowadays. For in our world Catholics are much closer to other Christians and Christians have a much closer contact with members of other religions. Correct information leads to mutual understanding and prevents intolerance. Moreover it helps us to a better (because a comparative) understanding of our own faith, and an ability to place it in the world of religion. If faith is weak this may lead to relativism. But if it is strong it will give it greater security.

Evangelisation

4.   Evangelisation, in the first instance, means preaching the gospel. Its first use is that of leading unbelievers to make their first act of faith. The evangelist's purpose is to touch the heart of his hearers and turn them to God. So he is not primarily concerned with instruction or teaching, although his message may well include explaining or arguing for his faith as St Paul did at Athens.

5.   Christ laid on his Church the task of "preaching the gospel to all nations". So the work of evangelisation has a permanent place in the Church community. We usually think of it as being realised in the foreign missions. We think of St Francis Xavier

in Japan or St Augustine's mission to our own country, or we may think of Mother Teresa's work in Calcutta today. For, as well as open preaching of the word, evangelisation includes the power of christian life and example.

Although we think of evangelisation as primarily preaching to pagans who worship idols, our main mission is to our own contemporaries. In western countries with a long christian tradition, a different kind of unbelief is very common. There are many forces in our world which are hostile to religious faith. There are many who are Christians in name but who show little sign in their lives of faith as a conscious act. Priests and teachers often come across them in parishes and schools. So the task of evangelisation — conversion of heart to God — is one that must go on in our Church community. Moreover, faith itself is always in danger. It needs to be constantly renewed. The conversion of our hearts and minds to God is not something that happens once and for all. It is something that must go on in us daily.

Catechesis

6. Catechesis is an ancient word in the Church. It can be broadly defined as "a dialogue between believers". Those who receive catechesis have at least a spark of faith in them; its purpose is to help them towards a greater maturity of faith, especially in the way of understanding.

It is important to recognise here the assumption of faith in both the giver and the receiver of catechesis. You cannot catechise a non-believer. You can explain your faith to him or defend it to him. You can preach the gospel to him. But catechesis goes on inside the community of faith. Often it is connected with important events in the life of faith. So we can speak of a catechesis in preparation for Baptism or first Communion or Marriage.

7. For the same reason, catechesis is not the same as instruction. Instruction, that is, teaching or explaining the doctrines and practices of the faith — is part of it. But catechesis attempts more than instruction does. It is not content with aiming at an increase of knowledge. It tries to improve the quality of faith itself; making it more informed and better understood and so able to get a stronger hold on a Christian's life. We ought not to confuse the words catechesis and catechism. The full title of our traditional catechism was "A Catechism of Christian Doctrine". This implied that doctrinal instruction was its chief concern. Of course doctrines must always be carefully taught.

15

But catechesis must include other things besides doctrinal knowledge among its aims. The object of instruction is doctrinal knowledge. Catechesis reaches beyond that towards a better grasp of those mysteries which are the true object of faith.

8. The two tasks of evangelisation and catechesis overlap. Christ preached the gospel to the poor in a simple way. He used parables from nature. He took examples from everyday life and work to give his hearers some idea of God's saving grace; to awaken in them living faith and hope, and to turn their hearts to God. To his disciples Christ spoke differently. They were already his followers. They already had faith in him, however fragile it proved to be when the crisis came. So he led them, for instance in his talk after the Last Supper, to a deeper understanding of the mysteries of his life and work. We see here in Christ's preaching and teaching the two processes of evangelisation and catechesis. In the work of St Paul we see the same two things going on. The simple sermons in the Acts of the Apostles arouse faith and lead to conversion. His letters have a different aim. Their deep, sometimes very complex teaching leads to a deeper understanding of the truths of faith and of what those truths imply for everyday christian living.

9. An instance of the overlap between evangelisation and catechesis can be found in the process which is sometimes called "pre-evangelisation" or "pre-catechesis". Our Lord compared his word to a seed, some of which falls on stony ground where it cannot put down any roots. Some of the powerful forces which influence children as they grow up today smother the idealism, the sense of mystery and of humanity's needs for salvation which usually motivate the response of faith. Often it is necessary to prepare the ground by trying to develop these human qualities. Especially in difficult social areas this may prove to be a long and arduous task. This pre-evangelisation is, in the secularised world of today, an important part of religious education. Better a well-prepared soil in which the seed of faith may eventually be fruitful than a quick but superficial and rootless growth of religious life which the first bad weather will carry away.

Religious Education

10. We have spoken of the difference and yet the close connection between evangelisation and catechesis. We turn now to the phrase "religious education" which is a much more difficult term to get clear than any of the others. It is quite a new one. We used to speak of "religious instruction" or "doctrine" or

"catechism". The years during which this change has taken place have also seen physical training become physical education, and sex instruction become education in personal relationships. The word "education" seems to have acquired a magical attraction. In what does this consist?

11. It is based upon the idea that human life involves a number of important fields of knowledge and experience; for instance the worlds of Science and the Arts, of personal relationships, philosophy and religion. Some writers refer to these as the "realms of meaning". An educated man is one who has an adequate grasp of each of these; who has the knowledge and skill to deal intelligently with them all, though he need not be an expert in any. Secondly, education has an important connection with the development of reason. It should help people to act reasonably, in an intelligent and thoughtful way. Thirdly, education should develop autonomy. This is a very popular word in educational discussions nowadays. It means that people should grow to stand on their own feet and make up their own minds about things. They should not be brainwashed into holding beliefs, nor should they be simply the victims of changing fashions.

12. This idea of education is not without nobility. Nor is it beyond criticism. Like most educational ideas, it is founded upon a certain ideal of human excellence, of what human beings at their best can be. It is too closely tied to the ideals of the modern liberal West, a civilisation with great qualities but with some limitations. To see these plainly we only have to look at ideas of education which originate in very different conditions, for instance in Latin America. Moreover, in its anxiety to emphasise reason and freedom, it leaves little room for the development of convictions and beliefs. Everyone should learn to be reasonable and thoughtful about these, certainly. But while reason can criticise and demolish beliefs, it is not so easy to see what it contributes to building them up.

13. The kind of religious education which derives from this idea is usually called "education in religion". Its aim is to give children an understanding of the world of religion from the inside, with sympathetic insight. But it does not attempt to influence their religious commitment. It is possible, the argument goes, to get inside someone else's religious experience without fully sharing it, to get and to give children the "feel" of it. It is no more difficult than it is for a good history teacher to give children the "feel" of Stuart England instead of a series of names and dates. The different facets of religion — its ritual, doctrine, morality, etc. — can be studied in this way. Examples can be drawn freely, from

B

a number of religions. So children might come to experience —at second hand but sympathetically — the Five Noble Truths of Buddhism, a muslim pilgrimage to Mecca and the doctrine and ritual of christian Baptism. Thus they can come to move freely and thoughtfully about the world of religion without being persuaded into any particular set of beliefs. This approach is attractive to a world where there is great religious diversity. It avoids the idea of "handing on a religious heritage".

14. This idea of religious education has much to recommend it. Its shortcomings are those of the theory of education on which it is built. We have some doubts about the idea of entering into religious experience sympathetically but without commitment. For religion is, after all, different from history or literature. It expresses our deepest convictions. It is probable, as Newman argued, that moral commitment is not a consequence but an integral part of religious understanding and assent. We come to understand our faith by living it, reflecting on the experience as we go along.

15. It might appear at first sight that this idea of religious education and catechesis are completely incompatible. But this is not necessarily true. For we can leave aside the uncommitted or "non-confessional" element, and something still remains. It is the idea that religious education should examine the different aspects of religion and enter into them in a thoughtful way; that it should familiarise young people with the main landmarks of the world of religion; that it should make their own religious beliefs more intelligent and personal. This is close enough to the idea of catechesis for us to suggest the idea that religious education is a particular mode or style of catechesis. It is the educational mode, the one which stresses the development of understanding, analysis and thoughtfulness in faith. There is no essential reason why religious education properly so-called, should not go on within a community of faith such as our Church.

16. To evangelise then, is to preach the Lord's message by word or example so as to elicit the first act of faith in others; or so as to deepen that conversion of our hearts to God which is the essence of that act. Catechesis is that process which goes on within the Church and leads the believer towards a faith which is more mature and better understood.

Religious studies deals with the objective facts of religion. Religious education leads its students to participate in, reflect on and analyse religious experience of all kinds. All have their value. In this book we shall be speaking mainly about catechesis and religious education. We have already pointed out (§15) that the two ideas are compatible with each other. So we shall not keep them rigorously separate. But on the whole, when we speak of "religious education" we have in mind a formal scholastic setting such as a school or an adult education class. When we speak of "catechesis" on the whole we mean what goes on in the context of the Church community; for example in preparation for first Communion or adult Baptism.

Indoctrination

17. Catechists and religious educators are often accused of indoctrination. Sometimes this is not a clear charge, but rather a club used vaguely to bludgeon them with. Still it leaves catechists feeling uneasy and insecure. It inhibits, sometimes, clear and forceful teaching. Therefore we should meet the charge fairly and squarely.

Some of those who use this word may apply it to methods of teaching. They mean that there are some ways of teaching which enforce beliefs on children by manipulating their emotions. For example, vivid and colourful teaching about hell could be used to shore up christian beliefs. It is not hard to create in children strong feelings of fear and guilt. Children might then continue to hold their beliefs because they cannot get over these feelings and not for any better reason. If this is what indoctrination means then we acknowledge that it is morally wrong and catechetically fruitless. On the one hand it fails in the respect which we owe to the child as a person. On the other it prevents that "free adherence to God in faith" which is the purpose of catechesis.

Others who use the word are speaking about the aim which a teacher has in mind. For them, to indoctrinate is to strive to close children's minds against the possibility of critical thought about their beliefs. It is to try to prevent the development of a thoughtful, reflective appraisal of them. Again, if this is meant, we have to accept the point. For catechesis, especially in its educational form, ought to aim at a thoughtful, personal faith and accept the risks involved in that.

But there is a third use which is made of the word. It embodies the view that only certain things can be taught forthrightly as true. These are scientific facts which are publicly accepted and tested, and skills which have proved useful. Beliefs, convictions and values are all subjective. Their truth cannot be publicly established. So all a teacher can do is to present them as possibilities and leave the students to make up their own minds.

This idea we cannot accept. It rests upon a confused and

oversimplified idea of truth and its connections with certainty. It leaves the development and formation of convictions in children dangerously vague. It is sometimes argued that it is a principle applying in formal education which is a public affair and should not therefore be committed on any issues which are controversial. Values and beliefs should be left to nurture and catechesis, to the private world of family and Church. But we have already said that education and catechesis cannot be distinguished in a black-and-white way. We believe that true education is perfectly possible *within* a tradition of faith. To put the matter in a nutshell: indoctrination is wrong. But indoctrination does not consist in teaching beliefs. It consists in the manner in which and the purpose for which it is done.

Chapter 2

Settings

18. We have described in the last chapter four activities which are often bundled under the general heading of "religious education". They all have some value. In practice they do not go on in isolation from each other. It is very likely that any religious teacher will be doing more than one of these things in his daily work. But it is important that he should be clear in his mind about the differences between them. A good teacher should know what he is doing when he is doing it. Otherwise teaching, or preaching for that matter, will become confused and ineffective. This is especially important because teaching goes on in several different contexts — in the family, in the parish and in various kinds of schools and colleges. Not all of these are suitable settings for all the aspects of religious education.

19. This chapter will offer a preliminary answer to the question: Which of the four activities we have described is possible or allowable or desirable in the various educational and pastoral settings in which our work goes on? It is only a preliminary sketch. For to answer the question properly would be to offer a complete policy for religious education. Here we simply ask: given that four different activities go on in religious education, and given that we have several different agencies for it, in the family, parish and school; how should the two seem to match up?

20. Two of these activities — evangelisation and catechesis — arise directly from the Church's nature and mission. However subtly it is interpreted, Christ's command to preach the gospel to all nations is simple and axiomatic, not a thing that we can argue about. The duty to catechise, so that Christians will understand their faith, necessarily follows if this first task is to be done.

21. When we think about the words "study" and "education" the case is rather different. These words imply scholastic and academic work with which the Church has no necessary connection. There is however a strong accidental link. Theological studies began early as it was realised that if the faith was to thrive, both a deeper understanding and a subtler intellectual defence of christian truth was necessary. Then in the Dark Ages it was the Church which preserved the classical heritage. Afterwards it found itself responsible in Europe for education in general. In this country this close connection between the Church and education survived until quite recently. To some extent it still exists. The connection was largely due to historical accidents (the "cleric" was the one who could read and write). Yet there were other reasons. Latin was necessary for the liturgy as well as being the language of general culture. Secular learning was believed to be a good basis for the higher learning of faith. The control of education gave the Church power in secular society.

22. For more than two centuries after the Reformation, education in this country was almost exclusively the business of the Church of England. The Church attached importance to it, partly for the evangelical and catechetical reasons mentioned earlier. But the additional reason that it was part of the Church's service to society was always present. The country came to look upon schooling as largely the responsibility of the Church. In the nineteenth century, religious pluralism came to be recognised. The Catholic Church and the Free Churches to a lesser extent, founded a large number of schools. Since both were threatened minorities, they attached great importance to the evangelical purpose of schools. They came to be seen as the main agency for handing on the faith and initiating children formally into the Church community. The schools were extremely successful in doing this. When the Dual System began in 1870 and the financial burden eased they became very numerous. Probably the greater part of our resources and pastoral energy was put into them one way or another. Other types of catechesis were developed very little.

23. From that date also the State began to play an ever-increasing part in formal education. It retained the evangelical and catechetical purposes of the schools in a rather watered-down form through the agreed syllabuses which removed distinctively denominational aims. The Anglican and the Free Churches accepted this and reduced their investment in schools. The Catholic community, true to its theology of the Church, made no concessions. In fact our commitment to the schools increased. So also did the importance attached in our minds to schooling as an agency of catechesis.

24.   In time, the approach to education in general became more sophisticated. As the idea of "transmission" lost ground and the idea of personal autonomy gained, it became more and more difficult to defend evangelism or catechesis in County schools. Many people began to doubt the value of school education for these purposes. At least they began to realise that where religion is concerned, the modern idea of education is at least ambiguous. A parallel to this development can be found in the connection between education and politics in the time of the revolutions at the end of the eighteenth and the beginning of the nineteenth century. Some thought that education would help preserve the social order. It would help the lower classes to understand the necessity and goodness of the social hierarchy. Others thought it would be subversive, and by teaching the working classes to think for themselves, spread dangerous notions of equality. So recently with an education developing critical thought and personal autonomy, it has been realised that where faith is concerned, education is a dangerous business.

Catechesis and Education Today

25.   There is a difficulty here which may be summed up in this way. We alone continue to use schools as agencies of evangelisation and catechesis while the educational ideal generally has drawn away from these things. This creates obvious tensions between our schools as parts of the Church and as parts of the national educational system. Especially it creates confusion about the purpose of the religious education lesson in Church schools. Is it quite different from the other lessons? Is it education or is it something else?

26.   We believe that it is education, and we already have given some reasons for this. Catechesis and education are not incompatible. They are in some ways difficult to reconcile in practice. But catechesis can take an educational form which respects freedom, encourages growth and personal development.

Indeed we raise this reason to the level of a general principle for religious education in our times. An intelligent, thoughtful, self-critical faith is perfectly possible and religious education should develop it. We must add though that this is not the only principle on which our catechetical work must be based.

23

27.   What then can be aimed at in our Church schools? First there should be a style of religious education which does justice to educational principles but which also has value as catechesis: that is, it should not only be concerned with a sympathetic understanding of religion, but also with the development and maturing of faith itself. Religious studies, as defined in Chapter 1, can be done as part of this. In our pluralistic world they are particularly valuable.

28.   What about evangelisation, the initiation or the building-up of faith in itself? In our language, the word suggests revivalist preaching. It seems to imply the deliberate manipulation of children's feelings, the creation of guilt or anxiety states, the attempt to close their minds against thought. It is always wrong to treat children in this way. It is an affront to their dignity as persons. But evangelisation can mean other things. We have already said that it can mean the witness of a christian life. It may be a by-product of catechesis or of religious studies. It may be an effect of the life of the school community. It need not involve conversion in the sense of the first beginning of faith. Conversion is a continuing reality and duty. Evangelisation also strengthens and increases faith (though it does this *directly*, otherwise we have catechesis).

29.   Plainly, unbelief and apathy, an apparent absence of faith among young people is the major problem of religious education today. So, Catholic schools cannot simply hold off from the question of evangelisation. We say in general (with some qualifications) that the classroom is not a very good place for it. But the life of the school as a christian community should have an important effect in kindling and strengthening faith.

30.   We rightly see the early stages of primary education as an extension of home. Therefore it can continue the work of direct evangelisation in the sense of introducing children to religious truths adapted to their mentality. These truths must be taught in a way which is rooted in children's experience.

The adaptation of truths must be very carefully done in a way which is faithful both to the truths themselves and to the children's thinking. This is a task on which a great deal of work remains to be done. At this stage too, direct evangelisation can occur very simply and naturally through the strand of prayer and worship which should be woven into the life of a class.

31. The primary school is usually closely connected with the parish. In later childhood, preparation for the sacraments of the Holy Eucharist and Penance should be done in close co-operation with both home and parish. The school's contribution should be the strictly catechetical one — assuming faith and moving towards understanding. The general principles of this catechesis we have already indicated. Religious truths must be carefully adapted in accordance with educational principles. Here contemporary methods of curriculum development will be useful. At this stage it is particularly important that children should come to have some understanding of the sacramental principle which is so central in our faith. It is also at this time that some important foundations of christian moral life should become established. In addition to the adaptation of truths and complementary to it, is the necessity to ground religious truths in the children's human experience.

32. Children should never learn anything which subsequently they have to unlearn. Nor should they learn anything which cannot grow; about which they cannot deepen in due course their understanding. In this way, although catechesis is for life here and now, it should also always have an eye on the future.

33. It is often said that religious education in the primary school is easy because the children are receptive, eager and uncritical. Problems do not begin until the secondary stage when they reach adolescence. This sometimes leads to the mistaken view that work in the primary school is simple, settled and doesn't count for much. In truth, to a considerable extent, what is done well or badly at primary level greatly influences later success or failure. Sometimes by eleven, children are already bored with religion, because they have been overtaught or taught badly. Sometimes catechesis has failed to be educational; what results is a religion which is static and leaves no room for growth; which is passive, unreflective, unconnected with the rest of life. Sometimes it is jumbled and without structure.

Those responsible at secondary level reap the harvest of these failures as well as facing new difficulties.

34. Difficulties in religious education in the secondary school are different and more obvious. They stem from two sources. In adolescence, new forces, physical, emotional and mental, develop within the child. He looks unconsciously for a new self, a new identity. He reacts, often, against the things of childhood, including his religious faith. Sometimes he begins to be critical, to see that reality could be differently organised, differently interpreted.

On the other hand, the social order begins to influence him more forcefully; the attitudes and customs of the teenage world, and also social and political questions. The religious world may begin to seem unimportant, unreal or dull. Positive unbelief, disinterest and active hostility all begin to appear.

35. There seems, therefore, to be a great need for evangelisation at this stage; especially since emotional conversions during adolescence are quite frequent and sometimes are an adolescent's means of solving his difficulties with identity. But adolescent conversions are notoriously unstable and direct evangelisation in the classroom leads to resistance and resentment over being "got at". Moreover, the classroom is a place for education and at this stage, respect for the freedom and growing autonomy of young people is especially important.

36. Problems in the secondary school vary enormously from place to place. A good deal must be left to the judgement and responsibility of the individual teacher. What we have described as "pre-evangelisation" — developing a seriousness about human values, a thoughtfulness about the human condition — is both possible and valuable.

It must guard against vagueness, superficiality and slavery to fashion. Religious studies are also useful at this stage. Their relative detachment avoids raising too many hackles. For some young people the religious lesson has not too much, but too little challenging theological content.

37. Religious education can include a mode or style of catechesis. The catechetical element — assuming a faith, however dormant or troubled — should continue. Often at this stage, it will be centred not on specific "Church" topics or events. It will aim at a christian vision of human life as it is and could be.

It will centre on the themes which are most prominent in adult human experience; on freedom, justice, relationships, morality, suffering and happiness. These "secular" matters are all things about which our faith speaks. Catechesis should try to find the ways in which christian truths can echo in secular experience.

38. In secondary school, much of the work of evangelisation — re-establishing and strengthening faith itself — will occur outside the classroom, in the life of the school community and in its extra-curricular activities. Here the reality of faith must exist not in word and in idea, but in shared life and action. A great deal of admirable thought and work is going into the development of schools as christian communities. It is a development which involves liturgy, relationships, community service, pastoral care and new forms of retreat and religious experience. It holds great importance for the future. Indeed the Catholic school has, in the deepest sense of the word, a *missionary* role. It should provide a setting of worship, faith, tolerance and care, within which decisions and commitments can be made. It should also strive to make an impact on the local Church and on the local community generally. The Synod of 1977 teaches that catechesis is not merely packaging. It should also be a dynamic and creative force within the life of the Church.

Joint Christian Schools

39.   So far we have spoken only of Catholic schools for which there must be a clear preference. For the most part, the same principles will apply to joint christian schools. Evangelisation will mainly occur through the life of the school community. Religious education should include catechetical elements with the opportunity to teach full Catholic doctrine. There will be difficulties in constructing the religious curriculum since the doctrines and practices of different churches are involved. There will also be difficulties about religious life and worship and probably in relationships with local churches. In all these matters, joint schools should strive to reflect educationally the present state of ecumenical development. There seems no reason why they should not make a major contribution to the growth of an informed and thoughtful christian faith in children. But the problems they present will make greater demands on the family and the parish to which the children also belong.

County Schools

40.   Religious education in County schools has recently gone through profound changes and its future seems uncertain.

Educational approaches have triumphed over evangelical and catechetical ones. We have already said that these distinctions are not simply black-and-white ones, and that the idea of education involved is not Holy Writ. It has been proposed that religious education should study all philosophies of life including those which have traditionally been considered non- or even anti-religious. No doubt those studies should be done, though we doubt whether there is much point in speaking of so all-comprehensive a subject as religious education. It seems possible that so wide a study of beliefs and values might lead to relativism, even to cynicism about them. Nevertheless, so far as this work involves the serious study of religion it is valuable for children. We ought not to be afraid of comparison. Truth should make us confident, not fearful. Clearly, in this case, the responsibility towards the children's faith of family, parish and other catechetical groups, will be much heavier.

Catechesis in the Family

41. A good deal has been said about the place of the school in religious education. This is not because it holds the first place, but because it is a complex, public and changing institution. We have always acknowledged, at least in theory, the first importance of the family. Phrases like "learning religion at your mother's knee" and "parents are the first educators" witness to this. The motto of the Family Rosary Crusade: "The family that prays together stays together" struck a chord because it emphasised the influence of the practice of the faith on the stability and formative power of family life.

42. It may be true that the strength of the family has lessened. Rapidly changing times and the pervasive influence of larger social groups sometimes create generation gaps. Very good families often find that teenage children react against the values and beliefs of their homes. Nonetheless, the influence of family upbringing remains strong and its influence in religious education crucial. Young children assimilate the habits and attitudes of their parents through the pores rather than through a formal educational process. They acquire their first knowledge of God, of Jesus and the gospel through talking and praying with their parents. The "school of the mother's knee" is the first setting for evangelisation. Again we must recall that by evangelisation we do not mean preaching or emotional manipulation. But inevitably these first ideas are associated with our deepest relationships. Whatever changes may happen later, they have deep roots in our personality. It is therefore most important that these ideas, simple as they are, should have a solidity and centrality about them. They should not be mixed up with superstition. They should not be of the kind where accidentals can be mistaken for essentials.

43. We have usually considered this simple indirect evangelisation through daily family life to be the main function of the family in religious education. In other countries, the idea of a more formal catechesis — from faith to understanding — through the family, is common. The development of this among us will be an important task over the next few years. We do not mean that parents must become like professional teachers. But we ought to help them to do the task mentioned in the last section — the first introduction of religious ideas — in a more systematic and well-informed way. Home-School co-operation is already developing. Support for parents in their catechetical task in the way both of materials and structures must now be provided. We hope that organisations of Catholic parents and family groups will take up this task as a matter of urgency.

Catechesis in the Parish

44. Unlike the family and the school, the parish is entirely a Church organisation. What goes on there is completely within control of our Church community. Traditionally, parish work has been chiefly directed at the Church community, though most parishes have been missionary in the sense of looking out for converts. Some are now taking a different missionary role. They are trying to make themselves corporately, and their members individually, more involved in local affairs and problems. The witness given by this is one form of direct evangelisation. The importance of evangelisation — the kindling and building up of faith itself — within the parish community must not be forgotten. Faith itself is always in danger today. Traditional methods of evangelisation, missions and parish visiting, need to be supplemented by new approaches.

45. But it is catechesis within the parish which is our main concern. So far as children are concerned, this has usually been left to the school. The catechesis of adults has been fragmentary. Many parishes have no school. In them, the whole burden of catechesis must be borne by the parish. This must be properly organised and supported. Priests should be familiar with and practised in the most effective catechetical methods. The training of catechists to do this work is already under way. It needs to become more widespread and more professional.

46. All parishes, however, have a major catechetical task. We realise nowadays that even the best schools have, by their very nature, limitations. In this day and age, however much better our schools become, the catechetical responsibilities of the parish must increase, not diminish. So far as children are concerned, parishes should support and co-operate with the work of the Catholic school.

This is particularly necessary on special occasions such as the preparation for and celebration of first Holy Communion,

Penance and Confirmation. Programmes should be arranged which will involve both the school and the local church community. Parishes should undertake also more regular catechetical work, especially with adolescents. The Catholic Youth Service has a broadly catechetical role and we hope that its work will develop in that direction.

47. Perhaps the most important single development in the next decade will be the religious education of adults. A great deal of this must fall on the shoulders of the parish. Again, we should distinguish the catechesis of occasions — marriage, childbirth, sickness, death — and the regular catechesis directed towards understanding christian living, morality, work and apostolate. Each of these has its distinctive style and methods. All are part of an educational process leading to a more thoughtful and active faith.

48. We will return to all these questions later. But first we must consider the foundations of our catechetical work. We will discuss its human subject, the person, the believer. We must give some account of the contemporary society within which it occurs, so problematic, so difficult. We must try to clarify the content of catechesis and the relationship between content and method; matters into which recent theological thought has brought new questions and some confusion. In all of this we ask most earnestly for God's grace and blessing, lest those who build the house should labour in vain.

SECTION II

LAYING THE FOUNDATIONS

Chapter 3

How do we become Believers?

49. This chapter is about the end product at which we are aiming, the believer, the formed and educated Catholic. That is an ugly and not very accurate way of putting it. For neither catechesis nor education in general is an assembly line turning off a mass product. Very little teaching of any kind is a purely technical, infallible process. Personal qualities and relationships almost always play an important part. And good education has a way of gathering its own momentum and taking unexpected turns. Nonetheless, every style of education gathers itself round some idea, and has some ideal in view. In ancient Sparta or in Nazi Germany, the only idea was to form tough, ruthless, blindly obedient warriors. Everything that was done from early childhood onwards was dedicated to developing the attitudes and abilities necessary for this. In this chapter we intend to describe our idea, and to sketch in the stages through which we grow towards it. We are concerned here with the development in faith of the individual person; with the stages we go through and the crises we reach. It is true of course that development is deeply affected by social factors, by contemporary culture and the mass media. In changing times such as ours these are the source of many difficulties in catechesis. We will consider them in the next chapter.

The Educated Catholic

50. The educated Catholic is one who has made a free and reflective commitment to Christ in the Church. This idea summarises the aim of catechesis as it is stated in *The General Catechetical Directory*. It explains why the *Directory* gives such an emphasis to adult religious education. For this kind of free and thoughtful choice is not possible for children. It is also a

C

very general ideal. In the next section we will analyse it into more specific elements.

51. We are going to pick out six aspects of this single commitment. Doubtless there are others that could be mentioned. These seem the most important.

(a) The development of the ability to pray and participate in the liturgy. A habit of prayer which has developed will not be mechanical, nor self-centred. Nor will it be isolated from the rest of life. It will be a prayer which has a contemplative aspect going out beyond ourselves. It will listen, as well as speak and so deepen the relationship with God which is its foundation. It will also gather up a christian experience of life and its problems into this relationship. Similarly, participation in the liturgy must go beyond formal attendance. It will involve intelligent receptivity to the word of God. It will also require an understanding of the Eucharist and the other sacraments and ceremonies; of their eternal reality and also of their connection with everyday life.

We put this factor first because it seems closest to the basic commitment and to the relationship which grows from it.

(b) The second element is a thoughtful understanding of the sources of revelation, of the holy scriptures, tradition and the teaching of the Church. We could call this orthodoxy in the positive sense of that word, for it is not blind conformity. It combines the reception of a heritage — the sources of our faith and its formulations; with a thoughtful, personal assimilation of these. In our world, with so many and such evident varieties of belief, a personally assimilated faith is especially important.

(c) The third element is active membership of the Church, a sense of belonging to it as our community, our family. Education always involves some element of "socialisation", leading young people into a particular way of life. We stress the word "active" because truly this sense of belonging should go beyond "being a member". It should extend to being the Church, actually constituting it and therefore being responsible for its present life and for its future. It should also include an appreciation of the structure of the Church and the principle of authority inherent in it, as well as that of co-responsibility.

(d) The fourth aspect is more difficult to express. It concerns the Christian as a person in relationship with others. For an educated Catholic, faith is not pursued in a lonely individualistic way; My Creator — My Saviour — Myself.

It is a faith which is realised in relationship with other people; these relationships must reflect, in their different ways, the gospel commandment of love. An educated Catholic is one who has a real conviction of his unique value and destiny in God's sight and in God's love. He accepts also the unique value of others and his relationships are guided by that principle.

(e) An educated Catholic has a distinctive morality. He develops the several abilities necessary for making moral decisions like anyone else. But two important differences mark out his moral life. The first is that while everyone has to live by his own conscience and often make complex choices, a Catholic does this as a member of a community of moral wisdom — the Church — which not only has a moral tradition from the past, but which is also a guide and moral teacher in the present. The second difference is that a Christian sees his moral choices as expressions of his love for God, as realisations of his commitment to Christ. Thus, although in him the process of making moral decisions may be the same as in others, the substance of it is different.

(f) Finally, the educated Christian must be able to translate his faith into christian attitudes and action in the secular world. The recent fresh emphasis and deeper understanding of the idea of mission (as expressed for example in the Second Vatican Council's document, *The Church in the World of Today* [Gaudium et Spes]) makes this element especially important. It requires a two-fold development. First, discernment; the ability to see and understand secular life in the light of the gospel. Secondly, it requires the ability to translate christian principles, the vision and commitment of faith into secular terms; that is, to understand how human affairs can be renewed by the word of the gospel, and to be prepared to act on that understanding.

Patterns of Growth

52. In some ways, growth in religion is bound to be similar to growth in other areas of life. As God became truly human in Christ, so religious thought and life is a truly human process. At the same time, we have to remember the difference between belief and faith. We can believe in many things — for instance in abstract principles or causes like equality. But faith is in the living God.

It is a relationship in which God is no passive partner. We cannot therefore apply indiscriminately what is known about the growth of beliefs and values to the growth of faith. We have to try to bring to bear our theological and spiritual understanding as well. We shall not attempt to cover all aspects of religious growth, but will simply express some key points in the development of the educated Christian, avoiding the language of technical psychology.

Prayer

53. We may begin with prayer. Young children have a magical mentality because they have not yet learned to sort out and apply the ideas of cause and effect. They are also egocentric. This is in no way a moral failing; it simply means that they have not yet learned to find a point of reference for life, beyond themselves. It is natural that when children first learn to pray their prayer will be marked by these characteristics. It will tend to be prayer for the things they want very much, to a God who is like any other provider of good things, only invisible and very powerful. This is in itself a perfectly valid kind of prayer. Our Lord said we should ask for what we need and that God would provide it. But it is also a limited kind of prayer and we should try to help children to develop beyond it. One way is to teach them always to pray for others. Another is to pray with children, spontaneously — an early form of group prayer — so that they can get the feel of prayers which have some purpose other than petitions; for instance praise, thanksgiving or acceptance. Many people believe that children have a natural sense of wonder. We can try to make prayer grow out of this, through the use of pictures or through actual experience. Although the mentality of young children is limited, their feelings and relationships are often intense. They can be helped to see that prayer is part of a relationship. In this way of course the quality of a child's prayer will depend on the relationship he already has. In this, as in other ways, his first steps will depend almost wholly on his parents.

54. Is it more helpful for children to be taught to pray in their own words or should we have set prayers? There is room for both. Spontaneous prayer clearly makes for a more real relationship. But set prayers may have the virtue of leading away from the limitations of early childhood.

Children should learn some of the familiar regular prayers of the Church quite early in life. They may not understand them. But there is more to prayer than the comprehension of words. These prayers will serve as an introduction to community and liturgical prayer when the language is necessarily and rightly more formal.

55. These considerations apply to early childhood and very largely to middle childhood as well. Adolescence is usually presented as a time of religious crisis — when doubt, apathy and alienation set in. But it has also been found in the past to be a peak period for conversions, when religious life establishes itself on a new level. Adolescence has been described as a "search for self" which involves also a search for values, even for the transcendent. We may not recognise these characteristics in adolescent children, but in a hidden way they are often there. Adolescence is also a time of heightened emotional life. Despite difficulties, adolescents can be helped to pray. Group prayer can be successfully arranged at this stage. Sometimes in prayer adolescents achieve the intense experiences which are important for them at this time of life. This is valuable in that it makes their relationship with God more vivid, their faith more luminous. Its drawback is that it does not always have much staying power. As idealism mellows into realism, as the difficulties of adult life begin to become pressing, the vision often fades. Habits of prayer (a dull idea) should be encouraged, as well as spontaneity. Something of the ways and traditions of prayer should be taught. Young Christians must learn that prayer is a pilgrim's progress, which leads through the slough of Despond and Doubting Castle before it reaches the Celestial City.

56. We should emphasise that none of these stages of prayer are expendable, to be cast off like old clothes. The process is cumulative. Each stage builds on the previous one and we all find ourselves sometimes (perhaps in moments of desperation) reverting to the very early stages, "Lord save me or I perish"; and there is no harm in that. But there must be growth, there must be development. We should endeavour to arrive, through these various stages, at prayer as an expression of a steady relationship with the living God who is at once our transcendent Lord and the ground of our being: "more sublime than the highest things in me, more intimate than my deepest self".

Knowledge and Understanding

57. About the second element, a thoughtful understanding of the content of the faith, we will speak only briefly. This is because it is the best researched and best understood area of religious development.

Generally, when we think of doctrinal understanding, the development is from an intuitive stage, without any grasp of the ideas and concepts, through a concrete stage, when the spiritual realities which doctrine refers to (for instance grace) are understood in a material way; to an abstract stage when it becomes possible to understand non-material realities. When we think of a child's grasp of scripture the progress is similar. It develops from a literal acceptance of the scriptures as fact towards an appreciation of their moral and spiritual meaning and truth. Again we insist that the quality of the earlier stages of thought is not wholly negative, unless bad teaching makes it so. Primitive religious thought may underpin a very real religious life. But good teaching must promote development towards the later stages and not cause fixation at the earlier ones. It is possible, for example, to teach the scriptures in such a way that their main religious meaning and truths stand out. These may be retained and appreciated when the stories in which they are embedded are being questioned or forgotten.

Relationships and the Christian Community

58. We will take together the next two points: that religious education should contribute to the development of a person in himself, in his relationship with others and as a member of the Church. Here it is more difficult to map out a developmental pattern. Still, since our faith is incarnational, human development must be to some extent a piece of it.

(a) We have said already that young children are egocentric in their essential mentality. That fact however does not rule out real and deep relationships. Nor should it exclude them from a real place in Church life. They can play some part in the liturgy and thoroughly enjoy it. If the Church seems like a large family they can develop a sense of belonging to it and depending on it, which may support them throughout life. We should emphasise that children are not pre-religious, and that they are true members of God's people even though they are not yet able to ratify that membership by personal commitment.

(b) We all depend very much on the groups to which we belong. We are to quite an extent formed by them. Small children are almost wholly dependent on the family. Adolescents too are deeply influenced by their peers and by the "Youth-Culture".

Adults may be less dependent, but they need support. No man is an island. Hence it is essential for the Church to develop communities and make possible a sense of belonging. Nevertheless, alongside or within these formative influences, there goes on the development of a uniquely individual self. With this process too, catechesis is deeply concerned.

We have spoken of the adolescent as being "in search of self". An inner self that we can live with, depends on values, convictions and meanings. It requires that we recognise that there are things in life which are unconditionally worthwhile things that are worth dying for and therefore worth living for. Catechesis is not psychotherapy. It is not primarily concerned with mental health, but with speaking and explaining God's word. Nevertheless, it must also and in the same breath, offer the convictions (not the ideas) on which good human life can rest. So it must concentrate attention on the unique value of each human person, uniquely loved by God. It must present the crucial importance of relationships as having their source in the life of the Blessed Trinity. It must affirm the goodness of the human world and of human life as guaranteed by the Incarnation. In these ways, catechesis must contribute to personal security, confidence and a sense of personal worthwhileness during the important years of adolescence. It must also offer or strengthen a conviction of personal destiny and vocation: that we are on earth to "build an immortal soul". In this way, as we shall see later, it should provide the dynamism and the unity of moral life.

(c) Catechesis should also contribute, substantially, to the quality of personal relationships. It is easy enough to see how this can be taught as an abstract principle: "love one another as I have loved you". But we can learn, even accept principles in our heads without their making much difference to our lives. Religious education (as a mode of catechesis) should concern itself also with the education of the emotions. It should find ways of leading young people through a process of emotional growth. Even done at second-hand this can be of great value. It can be approached through literature and the arts, through drama and role-play, through a creative use of the holy scriptures and the liturgy. The object of this is to help young people, not so much to understand the commandment of love in their minds, as to grasp it in their hearts and learn to cope with its emotional demands.

59. We turn now to moral growth. The development of moral thought and judgement in children and adolescents has been widely researched. Generally speaking it takes this pattern. It develops from a literal interpretation of rules, to their spirit; from the evaluation of the material impersonal content of human acts to an awareness of the importance of motive and intent; from an acceptance of moral rules as eternally fixed and beyond change, to a more flexible consciousness of them as contractual and to a sense of personal moral responsibility.

We can see a similar pattern of moral development in the scriptures from the Old to the New Testaments. In the book of Samuel we read that Uzzah put out his hand to steady the Holy Ark and was struck dead by God for the material act of touching it. Our Lord says in the gospel that evil things come from the heart of man and do not, in essence at least, consist in failure to observe external rules (Mk 7:20-23).

This leads us to ask: given that the Christian goes through the same moral stages as other people, what exactly is the religious dimension of the moral life?

We will say more about this question elsewhere. Here there are three specific points.

(a) Underlying all the stages of development is a real moral life. In religious terms this means that even if moral understanding is at a primitive stage, there can be a real relationship with God expressed in the choice of what to do. Although this is true, it remains important that parents, catechists and teachers should work to develop in children a more mature moral outlook. This may be done by avoiding over-emphasis on blind obedience, by giving and discussing the reasons behind moral choices and by highlighting the importance of deliberateness.

(b) Apart from their personal moral development, catechesis should help children to realise that they belong to a community of moral wisdom, the Church. Therefore, free autonomous moral choice can never mean simply acting for your own reasons, off your own bat. The Church has a body of moral principles and teachings (not a static, a developing one). These should be taught and explained. Again, the reasons for them should be given. What is being aimed at here is not blind conformity. It is informed responsible choice, but choice made within the orbit of Catholic faith.

(c) Although the religious dimension of morality does not alter the pattern of its development, it does change the essence and character of that morality itself. It places it in a new perspective. We cannot speak only in terms of the calculation of consequences, reasons and rules. Our vista includes the alienating force of sin, the healing power of grace, the mystery of christian hope and the judgement of God's truth. The task of the catechist as a moral educator is to communicate the place of morality in that world.

Active Christian Life

60. Virtue may sometimes be cloistered. It should never be fugitive. Most christian lives are lived actively in the world. Catechesis must concern itself with that world. It must try to enable Christians to understand the moral and spiritual values involved in social and political questions. The young child lives in quite a small world and this matter may not be of great importance at that stage; though it casts its shadow before. For the adolescent and the adult it is of great importance. He must never get the impression that religion is a retreat from public affairs into a private world of spirituality. Catechesis should teach discernment. It should also encourage action by offering a vision of the face of the earth renewed by the Holy Spirit. So, questions of war and peace and violence, of social justice and social organisation, of the rights to life and death, can never be optional extras. They must have a place in any catechetical programme.

It is always important to remember that from this point of view, the word of God in the Church can and must illustrate these questions. Catechesis must not remain at the level of a general discussion which never reaches conclusions. Christian faith must get hold of the whole of life.

Heritage and Growth

61. All growth towards maturity and freedom of choice involves a risk. Children may arrive at it and may make choices different from the ones their parents, priests and catechists hoped for. It is a risk that must be taken and for two reasons. The main one is simply that religious maturity is a good in itself. It is, or part of it is that "free adherence to God in faith" which *The General Catechetical Directory* sets before us as the aim of catechesis. Secondly, the temper of the times is such that only a mature faith will thrive nowadays. Even though we may succeed in building strong supportive christian communities, faith has to live in a world that offers it very little social support. So it needs to have strong personal roots.

For most people, only mature free choice can provide these roots. Young people learn in religion as in other areas, through exploring, trying out ideas and sometimes by making mistakes. Catholic religious education certainly hands on the heritage of the faith. But it must do this in a way which encourages reflection, even critical thought; a way which promotes personal choice in faith. We have elsewhere pointed out the importance in this connection of the idea of "tradition". Although tradition is handed on, it is not an inert body of material. It is something that lives and grows. We would do better to speak of helping young people to "get inside" a tradition rather than to think of them learning it as though it were formulas, facts or dates. "To communicate the type and allow for growth beyond the type"; that is the way someone defined the aim of education in our time. Slightly altered it may serve to define our catechetical work: "to communicate the faith and provide for growth within the faith".

The Educated and the Good

62. Growth towards religious maturity is not the same as growth in grace. This is obvious enough but it needs to be said plainly. The religiously educated are not necessarily the holy. Nor are the holy necessarily educated. Many of the Saints have been very simple people. The mentally handicapped will never be able to think about or understand their faith mentally. Many others will never be able, for instance, to grasp doctrinal concepts. Yet no-one can doubt that they have a religious life, often a deep one. This truth is most obvious in the mental aspects of religious growth. Yet it is true of other aspects also. Catechesis should help people to find themselves and cope with life. Yet to do that even superbly is not to be perfect in the gospel sense of that word. Christians, as much as others, often experience mental suffering, depression or anxiety. They often have problems of personality or temperament. They often fail in relationships and suffer through it. None of these things prevent growth in grace. Our faith is not a human success story. It certainly does not regard mental defect or mental suffering or immaturity as good things. But it does hold that there is a real — a redemptive — value in the way we cope with our sufferings and failures; in the patience and courage that requires. There is, as St Paul writes, a logic of the Cross as well as a logic of the intellect. We need to keep a careful balance here. The emphasis we have been giving in catechesis — the lines of growth it should promote — must figure among its objectives. Yet we must not allow this ideal of a mature Catholic to lead us to extremes. There are many tasks in catechesis which must accept much simpler, much less sophisticated objectives. There will be those who may never learn, so far as human judgement goes, anything more than a simple prayer or two. Neither they nor the catechesis we offer them is of any less importance.

Ideal and Reality: Degrees of Belonging

63.   All high level aims are idealistic. This doesn't mean that they are useless. On the contrary, they are necessary in all education, to give it its true direction. They must be held onto, but tempered with a sense of reality. The line of personal religious growth which we have put forward should be in the minds of all catechists. But also in their minds must be the realisation that in many cases they will make very little or very slow progress. This may be, as we have indicated, because of personal limitations. It may be due to some of the social factors which we will discuss in the next chapter. Catechists should try to understand the probable reasons for apparent failure. This will direct their methods of working as they move from general aims to the practical business of teaching. All catechists need a lot of courage, faith and patience. Our present world is nowhere an easy one for their work. They must remember that it is the world in which God has called them to work. Catechesis is a task, begun and carried through in faith and under grace. If it isn't that it is nothing.

Only God knows the truth about success and failure. Only he can judge a human life. So all external tests of success, while useful, should be treated with caution. There are degrees of belonging in the Church. Saints belong to it, but so do sinners. The thoughtful, well-balanced Christian who practises his faith and lives his life by it is at the centre. But those who have been baptised, have gone very little further and never darken the church doors, belong too. The link may be tenuous, but it is there. They do not stand outside God's saving mercy. Nor must they be left outside our pastoral and catechetical care. The catechist who can reach those who belong very distantly — even briefly, even without seeming to achieve much — is exercising as real a ministry as any other. In catechesis there is no payment by results.

Chapter 4

Catechesis in our present society

64.　　Catechesis does not take place in a vacuum. Some of its principles come to us from God's word and in the Church. But as we have seen, it will be ineffective unless it takes into account the patterns of growth through which human beings move towards maturity. We are all formed to a considerable extent by the culture within which we live. The word "culture" is used here to mean the whole way of life of a people, including the values and beliefs on which that shared life is based. The word which the Church speaks must be adapted to its hearers. This adaptation must include attention to the outlook, attitudes and formative influences which are dominant in the present world and in contemporary Britain. To adapt is not to diminish or to water-down. It is true the one involves the risk of the other. But it is an essential principle for the Church's mission generally, and also an incarnational one. Just as God became a particular man, so the Church must teach, as Jesus did, in the voice of its own times. All effective missionary and catechetical work depends to some extent on its ability to do this. Catholics should be more courageous and confident about it than others. For the Catholic belief is that God gives to the Church the authority and the grace to direct the process of adaptation, so that it can never go basically astray. "Faithfulness to God, faithfulness to man" is the watchword of catechesis. In this chapter we are concerned with its faithfulness to man in his social setting.

65.　　Because of rapid and effective communications, the modern world has become smaller and more homogeneous; a global village. There are more common factors and attitudes; more interdependence in ideas as well as in economics. So it is possible to make at least a few generalisations about "the modern world". Both *The General Catechetical Directory* and the Synod of 1977 have attempted to do this in order to situate the problems of catechesis today. We must not neglect national, even local differences. Nevertheless, we can begin briefly with some universal perspectives.

In the next four sections we will summarise what the *Directory* calls "sociocultural changes" which have "spiritual repercussions". We will identify some of the catechetical problems and lines of development which follow from them.

66. In the past, Christians concerned about handing on the faith have relied a great deal on the transmission from generation to generation of a cultural heritage. On the whole, this heritage has included, as an essential and unifying factor, christian beliefs and moral principles in one form or another. Nowadays, the culture which is handed on no longer includes the faith, even in traditionally christian countries. Relics of it remain, but for the most part these are of a superficial kind. Therefore we have to face the task of handing on the faith as one almost entirely separate from the regular "transmission of culture" which goes on, even in rapidly changing times.

This demands a process which is different from ordinary "socialisation" — which indeed will sometimes be in conflict with it. It also requires expressions of the faith which are less dependent on a particular cultural tradition; expressions which are able to root themselves in various and changing cultures. In most western countries, christian faith has been the unifying factor in society. In the democracies now the aim is not to promote a specific faith, but rather to encourage harmony among people of different religious beliefs. This is the situation often called "pluralism". It presents new problems and challenges to catechetics. For ways of teaching based on handing on a social heritage may well be quite unsuitable for promoting a "free adherence to God in faith" in a society which is religiously neutral.

67. Another profound change which has occurred in our world in the last few decades is the development in range and influence of the mass media. These, especially television, influence ideas and attitudes from a very early age. They do this not only through their explicit content, but also through the values which are implicit, rarely expressed openly, but deeply influential. Children's exposure to them is on average, very substantial and the presentation is very expert. So, when it comes to forming ideas and attitudes, the media seem often to be more influential than smaller more basic groups, such as the family, the neighbourhood or the parish. So a "common culture" — even though it is of a rather thin kind, — sometimes seems to swamp minority groups.

This is not to say that the media are a hostile influence. Their formative power has both good and bad effects. But it is a power which catechetics must take into account.

68. Most societies in the past have had, at least to some extent, an "other-worldly" outlook. They have looked to some reality outside human affairs — God or fate or Nirvana — for their ultimate meanings and purposes. Secular life has been lived and understood in a context beyond itself. This is no longer generally true. Nowadays, interest and concern is concentrated much more on human progress and on man's destiny in this world. There are a number of reasons for this. Prominent among them is the impression, created by rapid technical progress, that man will eventually be able to achieve unaided anything he sets his mind to. This "secularism" — the apparent absence of God from modern life — creates new difficulties for catechesis. Christian teachings, such as the existence of God and eternal life, no longer seem obviously acceptable; nor are they as urgent and interesting to most people as they were. But this secularism should not be viewed completely negatively, as though it were simply a hostile force to be overcome. It is the character of the world, in which we are called to live our life and fulfil our mission. You cannot put the clock back to medieval Christendom. Catechesis must renew itself in such a way that the relevance of the faith to secular life and secular concerns stands out plainly.

69. There are some places in the world where a traditional religious culture still survives and shapes the lives of groups of people. Here the task of catechesis can be seen as part of the handing-down of a culture. Its new task is to make sure that the essential and permanent elements of the faith stand out. Only round these can a faith able to survive the pressures of rapid change be built. In other societies, the faith remains only an empty shell. Many of the baptised have lapsed into indifferentism or into a practical if not theoretical atheism. Here the task is one of re-evangelisation. This demands a renewed presentation of the faith as well as the witness of a Church whose life truly realises it.

70. Having made these points, the *Directory* goes on to draw some general conclusions for catechesis. The declaration of the Synod of 1977 takes up and develops these. First it acknowledges the need for new expressions and formulations of the faith; specifically expressions which bring out the harmony between God's revelation and man's experience. Secondly, it warns against two dangers. The view which advocates more intensive and accurate doctrinal instruction fails to grasp the depth of the renewal which is needed. The view which wants to restrict understanding of the gospel to its consequences for man's temporal life courts the opposite danger. It risks replacing the gospel with a social and personal philosophy of life.

71.   These social trends are very broad and general. Bearing them in mind we will try to describe more specifically the social background to catechesis in England and Wales, picking out a number of factors which influence it one way or another.

A Pluralist Society

72.   It is certainly a fact that there is a much greater variety of belief and unbelief in this country than there was fifty, even twenty years ago. Less people profess orthodox and active Christianity. Many immigrants profess and practise other major world religions. It is said that in this country there are now more Muslims than Methodists. An awareness of the variety of religious belief, of non-religious beliefs and of disbelief is very widespread. The power and range of the mass media make it almost impossible to ignore the fact or be uninfluenced by it. Children come to realise it very early in their lives. So it is much less likely that they will grow up to think the beliefs they have been taught at home or at school obviously and self-evidently true. Comparison, questioning and criticism begin much earlier. So too does the attitude that everything is relative and nothing absolute.

A Secular Society

73.   The *Directory* speaks of secularisation as an outlook, a concentration on life in this world. It is also an external fact in the social order. Religion is gradually disappearing as the context of national life. It is true that there is still an established Church and a religious ritual which surrounds major public occasions. But the institutions of national life are less and less effectively influenced by this. The law, for example, no longer necessarily enforces or supports christian moral principles. The mass media adopt an open attitude on questions of belief and value. The education system favours programmes which are not tied to any particular belief. This last point is of special importance. For Catholic schools and colleges are to a large extent part of the national education system and are increasingly influenced by trends in it. In a pluralist secular society, the trend is to aim at helping children to think for themselves and stand on their own

feet in moral and religious questions; rather than handing on to them definite beliefs and values. Against this background it is much harder to see religious education as the handing on of a heritage.

Autonomy

74. Few words are more common in modern educational thought than this one. It is sometimes used to describe the state of mankind as a whole; "autonomous man". The meaning of the phrase is this. In recent decades technology has developed in a spectacular way. In the future, its progress will be even more dramatic. Already man has achieved a large measure of control over the material world. Through the human sciences he is now achieving a great deal of knowledge about the behaviour of individual persons and human groups, along with the ability to manipulate them. Some people believe that man has now "come of age" and that his control over the future of the race is, in principle at least, unlimited. Although this idea would only be expressed by intellectuals, it has become, in a less articulate way, a part of the outlook of ordinary people.

It is an outlook which presents difficulties to Christians as they go about the task of preaching and teaching their faith. Dependence on God, and a denial of human self-sufficiency are important elements in that faith. We are saved by a grace which comes from outside ourselves. Many theologians have, in their work, tried to come to terms with this conflict. There has been a certain retreat from the supernatural, a concentration on the light that theology can throw on the secular future of mankind. The work of Teilhard de Chardin and liberation theology both show traces of this tendency. It does not involve denying the existence of realities which are, in the traditional sense of the word "supernatural". But the emphasis is on a christian understanding of the things of man, and what he will make of himself. The things of God, the realities beyond the space-time world receive less attention. In catechesis, the use of human experience and the development of life-themes show a similar influence. Both in theology and in catechetics, the task of coming to terms with the contemporary outlook must be undertaken courageously. But this must be done in a critical and balanced way.

An Urban Society

75. Another effect of technical and industrial development is that most people in this country live in towns. Our lives are shaped to a large extent, by economic and industrial organisations. This has led to the fact which some have called "alienation". Work is most frequently no longer a real part of man's life, a part of himself. It is a necessary but regrettable condition of making a livelihood. So life becomes fragmented. The wholeness which religious faith should bring is more difficult to achieve. Moreover, we live surrounded by artefacts, in a world which we ourselves have made. This is even true of national parks and regulated beauty spots. So we are less in touch with nature as "given", a background against which we live our lives. We are sheltered from the forces of nature in buildings, umbrellas, heating, lighting, machinery, medicine, rapid transport. So they have come to mean less to us, the rhythm of day and night, the pattern of seasons, the earth and the sea.

Probably urban life has had, and is having, far reaching and deep effects on the development of religious consciousness. Again the clock cannot be put back. It is necessary to come to terms with this fact. It is still true in some ways that our Church bears the marks of, or looks back with some yearning to a simple, pre-industrial folk society. We have often been warned (for instance by the Second Vatican Council) of the importance of adapting our mission to the world which must hear God's word now. Yet much adaptation still remains to be done. Some catechists speak of their impression of speaking to a mentality quite different from their own, of a serious breakdown in communication and mutual understanding. We must work to remedy this. It does not mean plunging uncritically into the industrial society as though it were the only or the best kind. Our society has bad effects as well as good ones. We will argue elsewhere that one of the catechetical tasks of the liturgy is the patterning of life. This must involve in some way, a reinstatement of life's natural rhythms.

Mobility

76. The last half-century has seen an enormous increase in mobility, both geographical and social.

Before that, most people lived their whole lives in the place where they were born. They often had the same jobs as their parents and belonged to the same social class. Nowadays, a great many people move away from the place where they were born and have a very different job and social status from that of their parents. Hence the influence of the small, stable neighbourhood groups in which most children grew up, has greatly declined. The traditional Catholic parish was an example of such a group. Many parishes nowadays have to cope with a constant change in their

49

D

membership and this presents new problems for the parish in its catechetical role. In general, stability makes catechesis easier. It is then possible to think of it as the handing on of a heritage. Instability and change always make it more difficult and this is true of education in general.

Institutions and Structures

77. Movement and change in society is one of the causes of the declining influence of structures, institutions, conventions and traditions. Our world is geared towards the future. To many people, what comes to us from the past — the lessons of history — seems less important. So institutions and conventions are thought of as barriers to progress, as fettering human creativity. Spontaneity, informality and highly personalised relationships are much more valued than set ways. In the Catholic Church these structures have always — and especially during the last century — been of great importance. This is true whether we think of doctrines which are the mental structures of the faith; or Church order with its many regulations; or worship with its strict liturgical forms; or morality with its fixed rules and principles. The purpose of these structures is an essential one. It is to guarantee the continuity and identity of the christian faith as it develops through history. Still sometimes these structures are too heavily emphasised. They become ends in themselves instead of leading believers to the mysteries which lie beyond them. They can stifle growth in faith rather than supporting it. Catechesis must respect these structures. But it must also promote the spontaneity, informality and warm relationships which our times (like the gospel itself) so value.

The British Identity

78. In little over half a century Britain has changed from being one of the greatest imperial powers in the world, to being a small vulnerable western democracy.

This change has had a great effect on our national consciousness. Uncertainty about national identity means the absence of any national sense of mission. This tends to erode the ideals of loyalty, duty and service which were the best side of Victorian Britain. Another effect of this uncertainty is the vigorous emergence of the smaller national groups in Britain, Scotland and Wales. As the larger British identity declines, the smaller ones re-emerge. Their language and culture seems to offer stronger and more secure roots. In Wales, catechesis must take into account the national identity, language and culture in the broad sense.

In other areas too, which are not in any way nations, local loyalties have sometimes remained strong while national loyalty has become uncertain. Often this loyalty rallies round a local football team. This is one reason why it would be unwise to set out very detailed national plans and policies for catechesis. If it is to be effective in a distinctive local area it must be rooted there and a good deal of planning must be done there.

One effect of the relative thinness of our national identity has been a fairly widespread retreat into personal and family life and personal satisfactions. At its worst this has developed into what has come to be called our "materialism" or "consumerism", the competitive society, the rat-race.

It does seem to be true that a high material standard of living has become a major priority with us. Threats to it, from inflation or other economic troubles often lead to quite violent internal conflicts. It is not an easy climate for christian education. For our faith, while requiring a proper and reasonable self-love, makes also as its first moral demand the service of others and the frequent denial of our own desires. Nevertheless, if catechists courageously and uncompromisingly put forward the christian moral ideal, they will find that it is not without appeal and that they are not without allies.

Public Morality

79. In mentioning a decline in public morality we are not speaking of total moral decay; nor referring to the crusade for "law and order" which maintains (perhaps rightly) that society does not offer enough protection to its members. Public morality means rather that society upholds certain moral beliefs and standards and exerts pressure on its members to live up to them. These standards do not necessarily involve anyone being hurt.

They are simply what is generally accepted as right behaviour which should have the support of the law. Most societies in the past have embodied some moral ideal and reflected it in their organisation. The predominant view now is that society should only legislate about acts which are likely to harm others, directly or indirectly. The large sphere of private life is left to personal decision. Individuals must freely decide what values they hold and must rely on their own strength in living up to these.

Religious morality also values freedom. But the christian Church believes itself to be a community of moral wisdom which teaches with authority. Even so, we acknowledge that Christians nowadays have to make more personal moral decisions on their own. In a simpler, stabler world, they were for the most part, for better or worse, told what to do. Christian moral education has the task of preparing them for this responsibility. Moreover, it must prepare them to make decisions in the light of their faith in a world which gives them very little social support. Clearly, "telling children what is right" is not adequate. A new approach to moral education centred on the idea of christian responsibility is needed.

Social Idealism

80.   To speak of a "decline in public morality" could be seen as an unduly negative approach to the spirit of the times. We must set against it the strong movement for justice which also characterises them. This witnesses to a fresh, acute awareness of the injustices which exist both within our own society and between nations in the world at large.

It is focussed mainly on the different chances in life which different social classes have. It aims at a society where class will not count for anything, a "classless society". We can see this trend at work in education in the comprehensive movement and in Educational Priority Areas; also in the social services, in community development schemes and in projects for helping the old and the handicapped. As racial problems begin to make themselves felt in Britain, the same social conscience is sensitive to them. It leads many people to work for the elimination of the differences which exist or could exist between the black and white races.

These movements and ideals are not restricted to the elimination of material poverty. They are equally concerned with the cultural impoverishment which prevents people from realising their true potential, intellectually and personally.

Religious education is at its most difficult in those areas which are described as underprivileged. It must make common cause with work for social justice for that reason; as well as because the struggle for justice is part of the christian gospel itself.

Among young people especially there is quite a strong reaction against some aspects of our way of life. Many see and criticise the uglier facets of industrialisation. They are concerned about ecology and reject materialism and the "consumer society". Some would like to dismantle the whole of our social order, and speak of an "alternative society". It is not clear exactly what this means. But in general their hope is that our economic and social institutions could be broken down and replaced by others which would ensure equality and leave more room for what is spontaneous and creative. Young people especially tend to be impatient with what is conventional and formal.

81.   Recently, there has been a considerable revival of interest in eastern religions, Zen, Yoga, Spiritualism, magic and the occult. These all seem to stem from a desire for direct and immediate religious experience. They are related to the use of drugs to expand consciousness. Other movements such as that of the Hippies belong to this trend, even though they are less obviously religious. Affection and gentleness, love of nature and the body, intimacy in personal and sexual relations are common elements. Spontaneity and the desire for immediate experience also seem to lie behind the Jesus movement and the underground churches. Sometimes these have strong political overtones and overflow into the theology of liberation and revolution. Posters of the folk hero, Che Guevara, increasingly show him as a Christ-like figure.

These movements are important signs of the times. Yet it must be admitted that they affect significantly only a small number of young people. For most, the pop-culture of the times continues to be the strongest influence. In the absence of any widely-held national ideal it often happens that young people grow up without any conscious religious or moral ideals or awareness at all.

Ecumenism

82.   Although ecumenism in this country has not had spectacular effects, it has made substantial progress. Its effects on religious education are now beginning to be felt. There are some joint schools. There is more co-operation between national bodies. The projects for developing a religious education curriculum in County schools have influenced teaching in Church schools. More recently, the Catholic tradition of catechesis has begun to have some influence in the other direction.

There is one form of ecumenical outlook characterised by a rather superficial impatience with denominational differences. These are thought to be domestic details which can be swept aside without scruple. They are simply historical relics and obstacles to serious confrontation with the great problems of the day. On the other hand, there is a sober patient working with ecclesiastical realities; a recognition that denominational differences are sometimes differences about the nature and mission of the Church itself. The first of these two outlooks is probably the reason why it seems difficult to pass on to the young a sense of denominational loyalty. Education into and within the Church community is probably weaker than education in religion generally. Solid ecumenical progress proceeds from a position of strength not weakness or vagueness. When beliefs are held firmly and clearly, we are secure enough to co-operate with others.

Adaptation and Continuity

83.   We ought to take seriously the view of those who are opposed to the adaptation of the Church's mission and catechesis to the needs of the times. They object in fact that human nature does not change very much. What does alter is only a superficial façade. Religion should speak to people at a deeper, more universal, timeless level. There is some truth in this. We can still read Plato with profit. The fundamental human problems he discussed are still with us. Nevertheless, the degree to which human beings are formed by their culture is very great. It is hardly possible to filter out a universal humanity from its social, cultural context. To adapt to this fact does not mean to give in to it. It means to take it seriously into account.

A second objection often voiced is this. If we pay too much attention to social trends we shall lose sight of the Church's essential mission, which is rooted in the gospel. We shall run the risk of making the Church into an amateurish social agency, blown about by every wind of fashion. It is a real danger. On the other hand, we have to insist that the Church's mission is not static but developing. To try to preserve structures and formulations which have ceased to speak the word of God effectively is neither faithfulness to God nor faithfulness to man.

Conclusions

84.   If the preceding points are as accurate as such generalisations can be, the prospects for catechesis in these times seem rather bleak. The first question we must ask is: should catechesis be aimed *against* our culture? Should it be trying to educate a group of people who will be able to swim against the stream, to live by principles which are quite different from those popular in the world around them? Our belief is that the relationship of our faith (and its transmission) to contemporary culture should be one of critical *solidarity*. We live in our own times, we share in their problems and prospects, we are to a considerable extent formed by them. Their "joys and hopes, griefs and anxieties" are ours too. But this solidarity must be a critical one. The faith which is in us must enable us to see and proclaim those elements in contemporary society which run counter to the christian meaning of man.

The idea that one of the aims of education should be to help children develop a critical outlook has a good deal of truth in it. Yet no criticism which is not based on values and beliefs clearly and firmly held can be worthwhile. Christians have and must teach such a body of values and beliefs. Therefore they should be in a stronger position than others. They should be better able than others to develop in children a critical outlook on the problems of the world; on injustice, violence, consumerism, advertising, and the mass media.

We tend to be rather afraid of the ideal of education based on personal autonomy. For education in faith involves submission to a word which is spoken from beyond ourselves. Nevertheless, we have to concern ourselves with the element of personal acceptance involved in that process. Catechesis should help young people to make progress in their faith towards a freer and more personal commitment.

What is needed today is a faith that can stand on its own two feet. Some people interpret "autonomy" as demanding a neutral presentation of religious data so that children can make up their own minds. For the reason given above, we cannot go along lock, stock and barrel with this idea. Yet it is true that information, understanding and free choice are important elements in catechesis.

85. We have noted the urban, technological and secular characters of our times. The expressions of faith which form the content of catechesis must be adapted to that world. While not abandoning the essential christian vocabulary, it should build bridges between that and the language and imagery which is comprehensible and alive today. One purpose of this is to help Christians to understand life in terms of their faith. Religion should offer ultimate meaning and that meaning should make sense of all aspects of contemporary life. Another purpose is to make plain the moral demands of christian faith in the contemporary world. We must be faithful to the christian moral tradition but also take notice of the particular problems and moral attitudes of the day.

86. We must also be sensitive to the matter of social class differences. Religious teaching must not be too intellectual or too sophisticated. With many people (for example the mentally handicapped) religious faith will have very slight intellectual content. We must recognise this and not allow an intellectual élitism to creep into our approach to catechesis. An "adult" faith need not be a particularly intellectual one. Moreover, "adulthood" is probably a state of mind and feeling that many people will never achieve. We have to reflect on the educational implications of "Blessed are the poor in spirit". The ideal for catechesis is a common core, each unit of which can be developed to different levels.

87.   We must certainly be careful of the danger that adaptation might restrict faith to "its consequences for man's temporal existence". Many truths of faith cannot be presented in that way. On the other hand, christian truth should at every point be presented as relevant to life, giving it meaning and showing us how to live it well.

88.   Finally, catechesis must be sensitive to the religious trends which we find among the young. No doubt some of these are extreme or mistaken. But undoubtedly in others we find the spirit moving us towards those adaptations of Church life which are right for our times.

Our acceptance of these elements (meditation, folk-music, spontaneity, informality, etc.) must be guided by the golden rule; faithfulness to God, faithfulness to man.

Chapter 5

Theology and Education

89. The aim of theology is to make the faith comprehensible; to enable us to grasp it with our minds. It is different from Church teaching, for theologians are trying to understand and to explain, whereas the Pope and the bishops are teaching with authority. It is also different from preaching which aims primarily to touch our hearts. But plainly it is connected with both of these pastoral activities. Church authorities do not ignore theology, they assimilate and reflect on it. Sometimes they judge it. Preachers must feed on it too, otherwise their sermons become thin, vague and without substance.

90. So the role of theology in the Catholic Church is different from that which it has in other settings. It works within the context of the Church's teaching magisterium. So it has limits and that is not altogether a bad thing, as artists as well as theologians know very well. Moreover, it is strongly influenced by pastoral concerns as well as by the need to be as clear and coherent as possible. There is a good deal of highly speculative, sometimes rather wild theology being written at present, both inside and outside the Church. But we believe that most theologians have a strong sense of responsibility to the Church community. It is theology in their sense that we are speaking of here.

91. Since theology has a rather complex job to do, it approaches it in a number of different ways. Some theologians work on the sources of Revelation, Bible, Fathers, Magisterium, to produce a comprehensively formulated system, a "Summa" as they used to say in the Middle Ages. Others have a more pragmatic approach. They try to bring the knowledge and skills of theology to bear on important human problems, on the major issues of the time. The distinction is not quite a black-and-white one.

There is a theology of marriage, for instance, but since there is also a sacrament of marriage it is a matter which theology cannot avoid treating; but in that area, besides what revelation has to say there is also a large and complex human problem. We also hear of a "theology of work" and a "theology of liberation". It seems that the reason why theologians turn to these questions is simply because, like Everest, they're there and they're important.

92. The idea of a "theology of education" is rather similar to the theology of marriage. There is the fact, the necessity, the pastoral task of catechesis and this theology simply cannot avoid treating. There have indeed been in the past, attempts to build up a special kind of "catechetical theology". We also believe that there is a close relationship between catechesis and education generally, even though the latter does not concern the faith directly. Education, like work or social justice, is an important area of human life. Theology should have something to say about it.

93. The Church has to make many decisions about education; about colleges and schools, about the content and method of religious education and about its catechetical policy generally. It also has a stake in society and its future and so it must have concern for secular education. Without an adequate theological base, there is a danger that some of these decisions might be made pragmatically rather than on principle.

94. It is wrong to speak of "a theology of education" as though we have in mind some completed work. What we are going to do is to bring theology to bear on some important educational matters. It is the second, more pragmatic approach (see § 91) which we are going to use. Still, we wish to offer something better than a few vague theological reflections on education. There are several important questions in theology which have a direct connection with education and from which important consequences flow, one way or another. We are going to speak of three of these; the theology of the Church, the theology of revelation and the theology of faith.

1 — The Theology of the Church

95. The Second Vatican Council's teaching on the Church marked a considerable change of emphasis. It was not of course a change of doctrine, rather a development.

From time to time, new aspects of the Church's belief about herself come to the surface; sometimes out of her inner vitality, sometimes in reaction to cultural changes. The aspects of the

Church highlighted by *Lumen Gentium* and *Gaudium et Spes* are these. She is the sacrament of God's grace in the world. She is essentially missionary and apostolic. The idea of "mission" involves more than gathering people within her own frontiers.

It means also a responsibility towards the life and destiny of the whole of our race. Although an institution with an organisational structure, the essence of her inner life is that of an organism based on co-responsibility and charity. "The Church" and "the world" are mutually related; there should be no false opposition between secular work and religious life. Catholics individually and the Church corporately must be involved as part of their vocation in social affairs, in the major problems of the age, in the future of our race. Among these problems, education must be prominent. For if we take the word in a broad sense, it holds the key to the future.

We might describe this as a theological outlook rather than as a series of doctrinal propositions. But it does provide the theoretical background to a number of educational problems. In developing countries for instance, this sense of "mission" might justify the provision by the Church of education simply for its own sake. In countries such as our own, it provides the background to questions concerning the Church's relationship with the State system of education; the existence of separate Church schools and the aims of these schools when they are in some way part of the State system.

96. The effect of theological change on practical policies appears more clearly if we look at the theology of the Church which was predominant a few decades ago. This emphasised institutional aspects more strongly. It made great use of the idea of the Church as a "perfect society", an idea drawn from medieval legal theory. This led to a strong emphasis on the Church's rights and on the necessity for strict ecclesiastical control in educational matters. Concordats with the State were envisaged, but the attitude to the educational world outside ecclesiastical control was a defensive one.

97. The teaching of the Second Vatican Council does not depart from these organisational and legal aspects of Church life.

It does complement them with other principles which are highlighted as being especially important for our times. We should beware of excess. Some write as though the "mutual relationship" meant the dissolution of the Church into the world. They wish to avoid anything which could be labelled "divisive". They wish to interpret the Church's nature and work largely in social, even political terms. But the Council documents teach that this mutual relationship must pre-suppose the distinct and unique identity of the Church. This identity comes from God through Christ and is to be spoken of primarily in terms of the mystery of divine grace. The Church's inner life as well as her external mission is a reality that has educational consequences.

98. Educational policies and programmes cannot be deduced from theological principles in a series of logical steps. Many other considerations must enter in. Still, a balanced theology of the Church does illuminate some educational questions. One of these is that there is some truth in the idea that the Church should sometimes engage in educational work simply for the betterment of man. This follows from an extended, more universal idea of "mission". The promotion of human values and the improvement of the quality of life is directly connected with the kingdom of God. It provides a groundwork out of which moral and spiritual life can grow. Education does have an ambiguous effect. It does tend sometimes to develop an excessively critical and sceptical spirit and to destroy established cultures without always replacing them. But these are temporary setbacks. On the whole, the development of education, especially in underdeveloped countries, does seem to be a necessary phase in the evolution of man. When circumstances demand it, individual Catholics and the Church corporately, should engage disinterestedly in this work, even though the prospects for direct evangelisation or catechesis seem remote.

99. Disinterested involvement with education should also be part of the Church's mission in developed countries such as our own. No doubt most of the work, development and research will be undertaken by other bodies such as the Schools' Council and the Universities. Still, educational progress can be critically supported and the true values emphasised. Moreover, there are some areas in which the Church can make a special and distinctive contribution.

There is, for example, the development of programmes of moral education and of religious education in State schools. Here, because of our tradition and experience, we Catholics do have a unique, if sometimes critical, contribution to make. We should be prepared to enter into dialogue and co-operation with others whose ideas about religion and religious education may be very different from our own. The broad idea of "mission" which we are considering here would support our participation (which already exists) in the research of the Schools' Council and the Social Morality Council. Catholics must bring their own distinctive views to these enterprises and cannot expect that these will always prevail. Pluralism is a fact to be reckoned with. It is more than a mere barrier to apostolic work. In our "diaspora situation" it is the condition of present christian life, the situation in which God calls us to live out our vocation.

100. This same truth — that the larger sense of mission entails education for the good of society — has a bearing also on the existence and purpose of Church schools. This is especially true in our country, where the Dual System requires our schools to be both a part of the Church and a part of our secular educational enterprise. They have often to span two worlds. They have to be in some way responsible to both. So the responsibility of our schools to society at large amounts to more than achieving a minimum competence. It is more than the price of a concordat; it is connected with the Church's mission. It is partnership rather than arrangement. Our Catholic schools should participate fully, though critically, in the general tasks of education; they should speak up with their own distinctive voice in the forum of educational discussion. They should join seriously in the social purposes and problems of education in our modern society.

101. Having said all that — the Church is missionary by nature, her educational responsibilities extend beyond her own ranks — we must balance it with a complementary truth. This is that the Church's vocation is to be a community which guards and teaches God's revelation. So, besides contributing where possible to the education of all men, she also has to be concerned with the education of her own children into mature membership. Unless things are right in your own kitchen, how can you feed the world? Wholesale involvement in secular education does run some risk of dissolving the Church's work in a general wave of educational change and progress. This could destroy the distinctive contribution which the Church has to give. To preserve her identity, to transmit the gospel, to educate all her members towards maturity of faith — this purpose, though some might call it inward-looking — is essential.

It might be called "Church Education" as opposed to religious education. Or we might interpret it as another instance of the difference — and the connection — between "Catechesis" and "Education". It is the aspect of religious education which presents perhaps the greatest difficulty. A time of rapid change, both in Catholic life and in society, inevitably creates difficulties about the initiation of young people into an historic and traditional Church. Growth in faith depends on a personal commitment which did not have to be questioned when the fabric of society was christian. The question: What educational procedures will promote commitment within Church life?, is one which urgently needs study.

102. We have referred to the Church as "community which guards and teaches God's revelation". We must say a little more about the Church's *magisterium*, its teaching authority, so far as it affects catechesis. This *magisterium* is to be found in the teaching of the Pope and the bishops throughout the world on doctrinal and moral matters. Along with the holy scriptures, the liturgy and christian experience, it forms part of the content of catechesis. It includes especially solemn statements, such as dogmatic definitions. It also includes the regular day-to-day teaching through which the content of revelation is gradually clarified in the light of current problems. In presenting Catholic teaching, catechesis should reflect this difference. Infallible or specially solemn teachings must have special emphasis and prominence. In this way the true architecture of Catholic truth, its shape and pattern, will appear. This is necessary, not only to be faithful to the Church's teaching. It also makes for good learning. Teaching material is memorable when it is marked by order, pattern and coherence.

103. Catechesis then, must accord with the magisterium of the universal Church. It also takes place in a diocese and therefore under the authority of the local bishop. We have spoken of the Church school as "spanning two worlds". This means that it must be responsible to the local Church and to its bishop as well as to the local education authority. Other catechetical groups, too, are responsible to the bishop. The exercise of his authority however is not a one-way affair, requiring only passive acceptance. It includes an element of dialogue.

104. The bishop is the chief catechist in his diocese. Those who work in communion with him are his collaborators. He exercises his catechetical function in several ways:

   (a) Through his own preaching, teaching and pastoral letters.
   (b) Through assuring the provision and training of catechists throughout the diocese at all levels and in all settings.
   (c) Through keeping a watchful eye on the catechesis which is being given.
   (d) Through assuring the provision of, or giving approval to, the catechetical materials which are used.

105. This process includes dialogue and co-responsibility for:

   (a) The bishop is sensitive to the views and problems of the faithful generally.

(b) He listens particularly to the voice of catechists.

This is partly because they are close to young people and likely to understand their mentality and outlook. Partly it is because catechesis has a creative as well as a conservative function in the Church. The task of Church authority is not only to see that the heritage of the faith is handed on intact. It is also to ensure that individual Catholics, and the Church generally, make progress in a living, contemporary faith.

106. Finally, the theology of the Church today is quite deeply marked by the fact and the effects of ecumenism. This too has implications for our educational policy and practice. Ecumenism should be reflected throughout religious education. It should figure in the content of religious education, in the presentation of teaching about the Church. Both the historical origins and the present state of divided Christendom should be taught fairly, with understanding and sympathy. This must not mean relativism or the watering-down of Catholic tradition and teaching. Proper ecumenical understanding, relationships and development depend on a firm and clear hold on distinctively Catholic belief and practice. Nonetheless, what is held in common should be emphasised, discussion and joint ventures encouraged.

107. There is the prospect, indeed the reality, of joint initiatives by Catholics and other Churches in education at the level both of school and college. These should not be undertaken purely pragmatically for economic reasons. They should also reflect where we are up to in ecumenical development at the moment. They should be so organised as to leave room for distinctiveness on the one hand and co-operation on the other. Problems will arise in the religious education curriculum, in worship, chaplaincy work and general pastoral care. These should be faced squarely and can be solved.

2 — The Theology of Revelation

108. If the theology of the Church is the question which illuminates and guides decisions about the Church's participation in education generally, there are two questions which are especially relevant to the principles of religious education specifically. The first of these is theology of revelation. One central truth which Christians have always believed is that their religion is revealed or given to them by God in Christ. It is not a philosophy of life or a set of human values which can be discovered by human ingenuity or diligent enquiry.

It follows from this that methods of teaching and learning

which are appropriate when we are concerned with helping children to grasp or discover for themselves a philosophy of life, may not be appropriate where the christian religion is concerned. For example, in moral education today, a great deal of emphasis is placed on discussion and on discovery methods. It is thought that through these children can be led to make personal and free decisions about what is true and good, having inspected the evidence. Moreover, it is said that they can be taught the abilities necessary for dealing with moral and religious questions without being given any substantial answers. It is difficult to see how this approach can be reconciled with the truth that the gospel is given by God, preserved, developed and transmitted by the Church.

On the other hand, it is also true that God's revelation is grasped by men in a personal act. This act, although made under grace, can be examined and analysed. It may well be that some of the elements in it are similar to those which are involved in the learning of moral values and human beliefs. It may then follow that some of the methods of teaching which are used in these areas, can also find a place in religious education. Religious education is not the kind of evangelism which overthrows reason and disregards evidence. It respects individual freedom and promotes reasonable commitment and choice.

The point here is that if "open ended" religious education merely develops the ability to think about and assess religious questions, then it can hardly be called christian education. In that process, reflection and discussion may be promoted, but the context of this will be that of the Catholic faith.

109. How to reconcile the handing on of revelation with helping young Christians to make a personal and free decision in faith? Education in this country nowadays sees itself as "an initiation into worthwhile areas of thought and experience". It wants to minimise directiveness and maximise the autonomy of the individual. But the catechist, a "minister of the word" . . . must "stir up a lively faith which turns the mind to God, impels conformity with his action, leads to a living knowledge of the expressions of tradition and speaks and manifests the true significance of the world and human existence" (*General Catechetical Directory*). We are again up against the conflict which does exist between catechesis and at least some ideas of education. To be clearer about the meaning of revelation may help to resolve this conflict.

110. There seem, broadly speaking, to be two main strands in the theology of revelation; one stressing its objective and the other its subjective character. The first is characterised by the phrase "deposit of faith" whose overtones suggest a body of stuff, ideas, doctrines, teachings, which are simply transmitted from generation to generation, in the same way as Pythagoras's theorem.

This static view is not the teaching of the *Dogmatic Constitution On Divine Revelation.* That document acknowledges the privileged position of scripture in which "the ministry of the Word finds its nourishment and its norm". But it also teaches that revelation is a living and developing tradition: "God who spoke of old, uninterruptedly converses with the bride of his beloved Son; and the Holy Spirit through whom the living voice of the gospel resounds in the Church and through her in the world . . .". This developmental view, based on the theology of tradition, owes a great deal to Newman's work in this country a century ago. Its educational implications are considerable. For the kind of teaching which would promote the initiation of children into a living tradition is likely to be very different from that which simply passed on a body of knowledge (for instance, doctrinal or scriptural knowledge); and from that which aimed only at an individual inner process of conversion or belief.

This is still true, even though we acknowledge that the tradition contains within it elements of knowledge (e.g., doctrines) and requires the commitment of faith.

111. A more recent account of revelation stresses its subjective aspect. It speaks of "revelatory" communion. God speaks to the individual in and through his own experience. That experience includes the teachings of scripture and the Church, but these play a subsidiary role. In the foreground stands the individual's subjective relationship with God and this is something which he discovers in the whole of his human experience. It is a very broad concept of revelation and it is one whose emphasis is very different from that of the *Dogmatic Constitution On Divine Revelation* which is centred on the specifically christian revelation of scripture and tradition. It is an account of revelation common in the writings of "catechetical" theologians. Gabriel Moran for instance writes: "One cannot think of revelation as two compartments of truth, one natural and one supernatural; the former accessible to all men, the latter open only to Christians. The classical distinction between the natural and the supernatural retains some validity, but only within the unity of the relation between the one God and the one human community. In every revelatory moment, one might be able to distinguish a natural and a supernatural dimension. But it is through the whole of creation that the one father of Creation speaks to all of us".

This view of revelation fits well, perhaps too well, with the

E

contemporary educational theory. It leads to a curriculum in which the emphasis will be on experience and discovery, and off doctrinal knowledge. It supports the idea of "life-themes" in the religious curriculum, though it is not the only basis for them (for instance life-themes might be based on the idea of "interpreting the signs of the times" as that is put forward in *The General Catechetical Directory*). It is a view which is often labelled "humanistic", and indeed some of its expressions do seem to add up to humanism with a vague aura of divinity. Still, the case in fact is a good deal more subtle. It does establish a positive link between revelation in the Judaeo-Christian, ecclesial sense, and the broader sense in which "all creation speaks of God". The link is usually made in this way.

Central to the christian belief are the ideas of the freedom and dignity of man, the sacredness of human relations, the universality of grace. Therefore, central to christian belief is a universal concept of revelation. Lift up the stone marked "Open-ended religious education" and you find another stone marked "The christian doctrine of man". Lift up that stone and you will find another marked "The christian doctrine of God".

112. If we pursue this argument too far, we shall find ourselves in the middle of that never-ending theological problem; nature and the supernatural. But there is also a practical criticism that must be made of the "subjective" view of revelation. It is that if everything we experience is thought of as part of revelation, that concept is bound to become blurred and uncertain. If we try to make revelation mean almost everything, it is bound to end up meaning almost nothing.

113. These two views of revelation, while not perhaps theoretically irreconcilable, are very different in their general approach to religion and in their consequences for the religious curriculum. The most hopeful way of reconciling them seems to be in the theology of tradition as set out in *The General Catechetical Directory* (§ 13). Revelation in this context involves a developing process, God's word being articulated through various human ideas and in various cultures. Moreover, the traditional Church is seen as a sacrament, a sign whose effectiveness extends to areas of life far outside her own boundaries. The locus of revelation is the word of God in the scriptures and in the Church. Its scope, however, is the whole field of human experience. To enable children (and adults) to get inside revelation in that sense is a very different thing from merely transmitting to them a set of ideas and rules. The marriage of the gospel and human experience can be accomplished from either direction.

114.   Many of the things we have said about revelation can be said in a complementary way about faith. We speak of "receiving the gift of faith" as a grace beyond anything our ordinary human powers can achieve. On the other hand, we speak also of "the faith" as something that can be defined and handed on; a body of statements, like those in the Creed to which we give our assent as truths.

These are the subjective and objective ways of speaking about faith which are similar to the subjective and objective views of revelation. Again, we speak of "keeping the faith courageously", calling it a moral virtue; a matter for the will to choose rather than for the mind to recognise. Evidently, the idea of faith is one which has several strands. We prefer to think of it as a single, personal act — our personal response to God. Still, if we are really to make anything of the idea of education in faith we must analyse that response — that act — as best we can. This kind of analysis is bound to be a bit artificial. We murder to dissect. Nevertheless, it helps us to see what we should be doing — as teachers, as catechists — to help faith to grow.

115.   We might begin with the first of the three strands mentioned in the last paragraph. In what sense is faith a gift? And can that have any implications at all for religious education? Or is it just a matter of "waiting on God"? One plain meaning of the idea of "faith as a gift" is that it is our response to revelation; that is to God's gift of himself. This is not unimportant. It makes a great difference to the character of that style of religious education which takes the words "faith" and "revelation" seriously and substantially. It sets it apart from the kind which takes "man's religious search" or "the human quest for meaning" as its watchwords. Catechesis approaches its task already looking to God for his word and his gift. This alters its character and its spirit, deeply.

Beyond this, we also believe that the very act of faith itself, our response to God's word, is a gift, a grace, something which God's power makes possible. It is not therefore really an achievement of our minds. It comes from beyond them. Must we say then that catechesis can only propose and then leave it to God to dispose? Is it a case of taking a horse to water but not being able to make him drink?

Not entirely. Being open to God's grace, being able to receive his word, is not a matter of luck; nor is it arbitrary, given to one and withheld from another. Receptivity and openness are human qualities. The absence of them can be an obstacle to grace. Many believe, with Wordsworth, that children have an innate capacity for wonder — *that* things are, rather than *what* they are. It is no part of the business of catechesis to blunt that sense. To nourish it in children is to help them to be open to the gift of faith.

116. This theme of faith as gift, as openness and receptivity to God's word has another important implication. The main tendency in religious education these days is to emphasise free, reflective, well-informed commitment. It is a trend which appears alike in the phenomenological approach and in *The General Catechetical Directory's* assertion of the primacy of adult catechesis. It is a trend which in many ways reflects the temper of the times. But it is dangerous if it leads us to think that religion is essentially an intellectual and sophisticated thing. For the kingdom of God does not belong only to the adult, the intelligent, the competent, the mature, the mentally healthy. It belongs also to the little ones, the handicapped, the failures and those who cannot cope with the problems of life. And these are not just objects of pastoral compassion. They have a role in the Church, and sometimes — as in the case of the suffering and the handicapped — it is a particularly important one. They witness that God's grace comes through failure as well as success, through weakness as well as competence; that the dark side of life and of our world, though we must strive to remedy it, does not appear, within the christian understanding of man, in a wholly negative light. It is not outside the reach of redemption. Potentially, it is one of the channels through which redemption comes.

If we fail to see this, or if we give it only a notional assent and fail to translate it into christian thinking and living, we fundamentally misunderstand the nature of the Church. It is not only a theological truth. It is a truth of experience to which the lives of the handicapped and of those close to them bear witness. Equally, without this truth we are likely to make a fundamental mistake about the nature of catechesis. If we take its norm to be reflection and deliberation, cognitive understanding or even moral maturity, then we fall not only into an over-sophisticated concept of education, but also into a mistake about the nature of faith. Education in faith is a reality even for young children, even for the mentally handicapped. Their grasp of it and their expression of it is not likely to occur through the formulation of concepts, still less through the blind learning of formulas. It will come through the visual media, music, mime and especially in the experience of relationships. But it is a form of awareness, an unfolding of the seed of faith in conscious life; an unfolding which imaginative education can foster.

117. Faith we are taught is also a virtue. This means it is a moral act, something we do freely and courageously. So, educational methods which aim at moral development will be relevant to it. You cannot teach morality directly. Education cannot in the end really touch the point of human freedom. Yet we are not born with the ability to make free decisions fully developed. We have to learn it. We have to learn, for instance, how to foresee the probable consequences of our actions; what a moral principle is and how it applies to particular cases. These things can be taught and learned. Several programmes of moral education have recently been published which aim to do just that. They aim to develop the preconditions, the abilities necessary for making free decisions. All moral education which tries to do this clears the way for the "free adherence to God in faith" which catechesis aims to foster.

118. Although it is a choice, faith is not entirely a leap in the dark. It also involves giving reasonable assent to certain propositions. So it is important that the faith should be taught in a reasonable way. Religious education must make an appeal to the mind as well as to the heart. At one time religious education was over-rational — mainly the rather dry bones of apologetics and doctrine. Now there is a danger that it may go to the other extreme; that it may come to depend too much on feeling and choice. We must try to ensure that the ideas, facts and concepts of the faith are learned. This does not necessarily mean a very intellectual or sophisticated programme. The truths of the faith can be presented at different levels and with different degrees of abstraction without losing their essential identity. It is the "thinking through" that counts. Christian truths are often, in their official forms, very abstract. But it is possible to work them into a more concrete form while keeping them essentially the same. This is an essential element in building up a good religious education curriculum.

This aspect of faith represents its intellectual underpinning; normally necessary if faith is to be strong and secure. It should involve a renewal of the teaching of apologetics, a field of study which has largely dropped out of religious education in recent years. Even more importantly, the faith should be presented so that its inner coherence appears. Central things should be central, marginal things marginal. So the "hierarchy of truths" will be observed. So the faith will be learned in a way that has shape and order and this carries its own **conviction.**

BUILDING THE HOUSE

Chapter 6

Substance and Process

119. We have seen that catechesis has many aspects and takes many forms. It is needed by adults as well as children. It goes on in families, parishes, schools and in other christian communities. It must be flexible, able to adapt to the mentality of its recipients and to the character of different times and cultures. To highlight all this variety prompts the question: What is the unifying principle of catechesis? Adaptability and flexibility focus attention on the process: How to change, how to select, what media to use, what methods, what language? But what is the substantial core of catechesis underlying and unifying all its forms? It is true that all the different forms of catechesis have a single aim. This is to develop faith towards greater maturity. Yet beyond that, there is the need to get clear a body of content which is common to all catechesis. For developing faith is a process. Unless we can clarify the content, how can we be sure what direction this development is taking?

120. In recent years, the development of catechesis has been concerned more with method than with content, more with process than with substance. One reason for this is the idea of "child-centred education". This is the idea that educational programmes should be dictated primarily by the varying intelligence and the changing needs and interests of children. So the content — what is taught — becomes relative and subordinate. It is true that this idea has been influential mainly in schools. But it has affected religious education there and hence, indirectly, catechesis generally. There is a good deal of truth in it. But it does create a problem about content. If we were simply aiming at general religious development then maybe anything might be grist to the mill. But we are aiming at development in christian faith. That requires that the content be much more specific.

121. A second reason for the problem of content is that in the past we have drawn very heavily on the Church's doctrinal teaching. Nowadays it is less easy to do that.

This is partly because there is at present a good deal of rather drastic theological speculation. Moreover, at one time most people heard very little about what the theologians were saying. They wrote for a small, scholarly and critical audience. Now the media quickly pick up new theological ideas. Especially if they seem excitingly different, they are likely to be widely broadcast. This has the effect of seeming to undermine doctrinal certainties. As far as content goes, many religious educators simply do not know where they are.

122. A third development which creates some difficulty is that the official teaching of the Church has recently been cast much less often in the form of exact formulas which are approved or condemned. It has used much more the language of scripture and experience. This difference is very plain when we look at the most substantial and solemn body of the Church teaching of recent years, that of the Second Vatican Council. The reasons for this are clear enough. The teaching of the Council speaks to us more personally and vividly — not to our minds alone. It has a broader, more pastoral purpose. But it creates difficulties for the content of catechesis if we are trying to extract from it little nuggets of doctrine which will form the content of catechesis. We shall show in the next chapter that to reduce that content to doctrinal formulas is not the right approach.

123. Content and method cannot be wholly separated as though content were the substance and method simply packaging. It is not possible to filter out a body of pure content to be kept in a cool dry germ-free place. The two affect each other in the process of catechesis and in the light of its aims. The purpose of catechesis is to develop faith towards maturity especially along the path of understanding. With this in view, it will be necessary to select content and shape it. It will be necessary to devise and adapt methods. The medium is not the message. But medium and message are so closely connected that it is never possible to keep them wholly separate.

123. Nevertheless, it is true that in recent years there has been an excessive emphasis on method or "approach". Problems of motivation, apathy and indifference have led to a constant search for new ways and techniques. Consequently, there has been less interest in the content of catechesis, and less care has been taken with it. This might not matter if we were only concerned to help people to become more thoughtful and sensitive about religion.

Any material could be used for that purpose. But we are also committed to handing on the heritage of the christian faith. Therefore it is essential that we formulate the content of that faith as clearly as possible. We also have to make sure that content has its proper influence as the process of catechesis. It must not only be there, it must also play its part in shaping the way we teach. "Method", motivation, developmental stages and intelligence influence the selection of content. But the converse of this is also true. The character of the material, its key ideas, its ways of thought must also have an influence on the methods that are used.

Chapter 7

The content of Catechesis

125. It is now clear then that planning religious education is not a matter of separating out a body of "pure content" and then setting out to teach it. This is mistaken for, as we have shown, "content" is always governed by our aims. When we have said as clearly as we can, what these are, we will have to select and shape teaching material in the light of them. The process of teaching and learning is a unity as in other subjects. Moreover, as we have shown earlier, one purpose of religious education for Christians is the handing on of revelation. And one aspect of revelation is God's self-communication to a person within his own experience. Content therefore must always be related to personal religious development and to personal needs. One person may thrive on a diet rich in theology and intellectual foundations of the faith. Another will not be able to take this. Other ways of expressing the faith must be found for him.

126. Nevertheless, if we are to teach religion formally, we do need a body of material; just as in teaching history or physics we need to be able to state the key ideas and methods of the subject. We have said already that while you can take "religion" in a detached and academic way, there is also a case for saying that the true learning of religion requires a moral and personal commitment. And this is the view we take here in proposing a brief summary of the content of religious education.

127. These things being said, what is the content of religious education? We begin with the statement of *The General Catechetical Directory* that it is the *mysteries* of our faith; and specifically that it is the four key mysteries of the Trinity, the Incarnation and Redemption, the Spirit and the Church. But what is meant by "teaching a mystery"? Is it not essentially unlike the

76

Second Law of Thermodynamics and essentially unteachable? We accept that you cannot learn a mystery as though it were an ordinary piece of cognitive learning — the principle of quadratic equations or the probable causes of the Hundred Years War. Nevertheless, for the christian understanding of life, a mystery is not — like mystery tours or novels — something whose purpose is to be puzzling. It is the expression of a truth of such richness and depth that it cannot be expressed in discursive, step-by-step terms.

A mystery is not meant to be understood in a comprehensive, totally logical way. Yet — "mysterium fidei" — it is the mental essence of christian life. If we cannot speak of "learning" the mysteries of faith step by step, we must find some other way of approaching them systematically. We have said, in discussing the theology of revelation in relation to religious education, that the "terminus" of an educated faith is not propositions but realities. Yet propositions — the ways in which faith is articulated — the sacred books, the ceremonies, the doctrines, are essential if the grasp of mystery is to be more than a cloudy intuition. These expressions, the mediating statements, are not learned for their own sake. They are learned because they open the way to and afford a guarantee of, realities which certainly lie beyond them. They must be taught in the light of this principle.

128. When we think or speak of "learning" the mysteries of the faith, we do not mean learning them step by step as one might learn a table in arithmetic. We mean promoting a penetration into them. We mean that these mysteries will govern our teaching of the faith, even though the material we use may not directly express them. If this is not achieved, then our teaching of the faith will not be truthful. Doctrinal statements and moral rules must be and must be seen to be related to the realities which lie behind them. If they are not that they will be educationally and religiously useless, indeed positively harmful.

After these introductory points, we must try to say, as clearly as possible, what the content of religious education is. Many people identify it with doctrinal correctness. Although we believe that good doctrinal teaching has been neglected over the last few years, we hope that we have said enough to make plain that doctrine is not the only nor even the first language of faith. Therefore, we are not taking as our framework a doctrinal synthesis such as the Nicene Creed, or Pope Paul's Credo of the people of God. We propose to fall back on an old and well established idea. It is that there are four "great ways" or four "content areas" in religious education. These are scripture, doctrine, liturgy and life-experience. Each of these, in its own distinctive way, offers a point of entry towards the mysteries which lie at the heart of our faith.

1 — *Unless Some Man Show Me*

129. In one form or another, the holy scriptures have always been regarded as an essential element in christian religious education. This is true whether we think of catechesis in the early Church or of the "Bible without note or comment" of the nineteenth century Agreed Syllabuses. There has been in recent years a certain movement against the use of the scriptures in religious education. They are sometimes said to be culturally too distant. Or it is argued (and we have already met this point) that they restrict education too much to one tradition of faith. We propose now to try to answer the question: Why should we use the scriptures in religious education? How can we meet the difficulties they raise?

130. The first reason we give for insisting on the use of holy scriptures in religious education is that they are the word of God in a sense in which no other human writing is. They are normative. They have a permanence and centrality which force the developing Church in everything it does and says, to look back to the holy scriptures as a rule or foundation against which it measures itself. To say this is not to espouse a fundamentalist view of scripture. On the contrary, the more we discover about the language and the literary form of the ancient Middle East, the more effectively is the meaning of scripture revealed to us: the more powerfully does it become a norm or rule against which we can measure the development of our religious life and thought.

131. The scriptures always have been a guide and source for theology, for the better formulation of christian truth. They have also nourished the personal and spiritual lives of the faithful. If it is asked why ordinary Christians, apart from those professionally concerned with religious studies, should have some understanding of scripture, this is the answer we must give. We can put it more specifically and say that some understanding of scripture is necessary for the sake of the celebration of the liturgy. For the word of God in its scriptural form makes up a substantial part of the liturgy. If we are serious about liturgical renewal, about promoting active liturgical participation, then some ability to understand the word of God in scripture must be a part of our religious education.

132. We have to meet the objection that the world of the Bible is culturally remote from our times. It is true that this fact raises many difficulties. In our industrial society, in our man-made world, the language and imagery of the scriptures do not come alive very easily. However, one of the functions of education is to liberate people from the limitations of their own times. Good history and geography teachers, radio and T.V. programmes can present the remote past and the remote present very effectively. Moreover, if we consider the immense variety of material within the Bible — take for example the Genesis story, the Psalms, the Song of Songs, Ecclesiastes, St John's Gospel, the letters to the Corinthians and the Apocalypse — the charge of irrelevance does not stand up very well. There are few, if any, aspects of life which are not touched upon. There are of course many problems involved in the use of the Bible in education. But they are problems of method and presentation rather than of principle.

133. We must still ask: What is our aim in using the holy scriptures in religious education? They are a unique source for grasping and penetrating the ultimate mysteries of our faith. How is this likely to be achieved through these rather remote and difficult writings? It is not enough simply to say that God's word has a power of its own. We must try to show also how this power works through human minds and voices.

134. The old idea of "Bible History", simply knowledge of biblical events and persons, is not without value. An understanding of the Bible does require some knowledge of the ancient Near East. You need to know what a Samaritan was and something about the Passover: have some knowledge of St Paul's life and work and some idea about the difference between the first three gospels and the fourth. You need some understanding of the kinds of writing there are in the Bible; and this can be put quite simply and need not involve any scholarly study of literary forms.

135. All the same, scripture knowledge of this kind is primarily a matter of removing obstacles to understanding. It opens the way for the Bible to do its real work. What is this? It has three main aspects.

136. The word of God in scripture acts not only on our minds but on our hearts. It is formative as well as informative. Therefore to teach it or to learn it (we might say "scriptural education") cannot be restricted to knowledge and ideas. We should have a method of teaching which enables learners to respond to God's word in it: rather as we respond to a poem, or a novel (and indeed there are both poems and stories in the Bible).

Good teaching should enable us to feel our way into the Bible text as well as knowing its meaning: to respond to it emotionally as well as mentally; and to respond in faith. Behind this is the ancient truth that the scriptures yield up their secret to us (or take hold of us) if they are approached reflectively and prayerfully. "Meditating" on the scriptures has always been an essential part of christian spirituality. A modern variant of it is the "Gospel Enquiry" developed by the late Cardinal Cardijn. We should develop methods of teaching which are in this tradition. A good poetry teacher offers an example. He does not concern himself (except secondarily) with grammar or syntax or scansion or rhyme. He tries to enable his pupils to find a foothold in the poem so that they can get into the experience which it expresses. When the Ethiopian put the question, "How can I understand unless some man show me?" the deacon Philip did not reply with biblical archaeology or Hebrew roots. He "explained the Good News of Jesus to him". He opened the scriptures to him as did Jesus himself to the disciples on the road to Emmaus.

137. The second aspect of the educational work of scripture can be summed up in the phrase, "Salvation History". At one time this was thought to be the main idea and structure of religious education. Few people hold that any longer, but still the idea retains its importance. It is that God reveals himself not only through words and ideas but also through acts: not only through the calm abstract schemes of philosophy, but also through the vivid hurly-burly of history. No doubt the finger of God can be detected in all the history of our race, but they appear in a special and privileged way in the history of Israel, of Christ and of the Church. Here is the record of a special relationship, a covenant, a choice. It unrolls in the individual biographies like that of David or Esther and in the social history of Israel's faltering but never dying efforts to reflect God's justice. It appears in the sweep and shape of that nation's history, its movements towards a climax, its hope. It is there in the social reforms and the poetry of the Prophets, in Job's wrestling with the problem of evil, in the faithfulness of Abraham, the protest songs of the Exile, the passionate zeal of Paul. All human life is there. It is as much about God's dealings with us as it is about old unhappy far-off things and battles of long ago. No doubt it is hard to teach this unless you are yourself penetrated by the power of the scriptures. But modern methods in history teaching offer helpful examples.

138. Thirdly, we should say something about the variety of material in the scriptures. There is not much educational potential in the book of Leviticus. There is a difference between the Old Testament and the New. Among the scriptures, for Christians, the gospels hold a specially privileged place. This is simply because they present to us openly and directly the person and teaching of the Lord. One major aim in all our educational and pastoral work is to help others to know and to love Christ. It is true that, in faith, Christians detect the presence of Christ in all their experience, in the whole world and especially in other people.

> "Christ prays in ten thousand places
> Lovely in limbs and lovely in eyes not his
> To the Father through the features of men's faces...".

Yet how is this knowledge and love to grow unless Christ is present to us as a person? And how shall we know that life, personality and teaching unless we have read the gospels reflectively and with some understanding? There is no need to introduce complex arguments about which are the actual words of Jesus or in what sense the gospels are an eye witness account. It is enough to start from the principle that they are the authentic witness to the life and teaching of Jesus of those who knew him. In all forms of religious education, imaginative teaching of the gospels should have a special place.

139. St Paul tells us that "all scripture is inspired by God and can profitably be used for teaching, for refuting error, for guiding people's lives and teaching them to be holy" (II Tim 3:16). The purpose of scripture in catechesis is to enable it to do these things. We must find the methods and approaches which will enable the inner power of the scriptures to be realised. As we have suggested already, the methods used in teaching literature and history and the technique of the gospel enquiry suggest useful ways of working. We also recommend the development of biblical themes in which key ideas — Covenant, Kingdom etc. are studied. They offer a way in which the whole texture and movement of the scriptures can be grasped.

2 — Truths and Consequences

Doctrine as Content

140. Faith goes beyond rational understanding. Yet the impulse of faith to "seek for understanding" as St Anselm put it, is a sound one. It results in a doctrinal system. Faith is a leap beyond the limits of argument. Yet giving "reasons for the hope that is within us" is natural and necessary. It leads to apologetics. Apologetics never causes faith the way a legal argument may

F

cause conviction. Doctrine never comprehends the mysteries of our faith exhaustively, the way we might comprehend a theorem in geometry. But between them they make up the main rational element in religion. Christians are called always, but especially in times of change, to explain and defend their faith clearly and effectively. Indeed the original meaning of the word "doctrine" was precisely "what is teachable" in the faith.

Western Catholicism has been outstandingly the Church of doctrine; sometimes even, excessively speculative, excessively rational. In recent years doctrine has been less emphasised in preaching and in teaching. Scriptural and liturgical renewals have made these idioms of faith stronger. It is a time of considerable and radical theological speculation which leaves some people feeling that they do not know where they are when it comes to formulating christian truth. The Second Vatican Council, a source of so much of our religious life and renewal, was not doctrinal but pastoral in its teaching. In some areas — notably in religious education — the eclipse of doctrine seems to have produced a certain thinness of substance. It is not so much that people disbelieve doctrine as that they tend to leave it alone.

Many years have passed now since the Council. Waves of change have broken over the world of religious education. After these years it is time to take a fresh look at the place of doctrine in our religious education. This is not a plea for a return to the catechism any more than concern about basic skills is a plea for a return to drill and parrot learning.

It is not a question of putting more doctrine in the package, the way we might put more meat in sausages. The different elements in the content of religious education are not like the ingredients of a dish which can be added or subtracted simply to improve the flavour.

Each of them — and this applies equally to scripture, liturgy and history — has its own special function and value. A good catechesis is one which recognises and makes the most of that function and value. A reconsideration of the place of doctrine in religious education must begin with the questions: What is the place of doctrine in the birth and growth of christian life? What does it offer to the Church and the individual Christian? How does it help us to know the doctrine of the Incarnation as well as loving and following Jesus? Why should we not only feel compunction, but know its definition as well?

What Doctrine is Not

141. Doctrine is not a description of what is the case, like the formulas of chemistry or the laws of physics. Because doctrines are often cast in the form of propositions, X=Y, they may look like that. It is this similarity which misleads some people into thinking that doctrine is the real hard stuff of religion on which we build the other elements, like marzipan and icing on a cake. But this resemblance is one of form rather than substance. Our doctrines are doctrines of the faith. It is out of faith that they grow and against faith that they are measured. They are not, therefore, like the formulas of science, the product of a process of observation, hypothesis, verification and conclusion.

Doctrines are not the object of faith. They do not give, have never pretended to give, an exhaustive account of that object. The realities which are the true object of faith, are mysteries. These are not puzzles or enigmas but realities which lie, by their very nature, beyond rational expression in human words. Doctrines have a secondary or subsidiary function in relation to these realities. It is important to remember this truth, both in accepting and in teaching doctrines. If they are themselves elevated into objects of faith, they can easily become idols which block our road into the realities of faith rather than opening it up. In a similar way, if moral rules are mistaken for the whole of morality, they can thwart their own purpose. The Pharisees in our Lord's day made an idol of the law. It blinded them to the reality of their relationship with God. When children are taught to read badly they sometimes develop a verbal façade.

They learn to use words without grasping meanings and this superficial achievement can block further learning. We also find sometimes, a doctrinal façade, a superficial knowledge of propositions which closes the road to religious reality.

Doctrines should be taught for what they are, one way of arriving safely and truly at the mysteries of faith.

It is because of their subsidiary function that doctrines can and do develop. If they were the real stuff of faith they never could. But in fact, doctrine is a continuous, a never-ending effort to express what can never be finally and adequately formulated. Some awareness of this continuous development should from the beginning be woven into our doctrinal understanding.

What is Doctrine?

142. Doctrine is an expression of the substance of faith which can be grasped by the mind. It is an expression of faith which uses the forms of knowledge. It uses a language as exact and well-defined as possible to develop a system of ideas which is clear and well unified. So it is a very different language of faith from that which we find in scripture and liturgy, both of which appeal to feeling and imagination.

Doctrine excludes these and speaks to the head rather than to the heart. This is not because mental understanding is the essence of religion. But as we have seen it has a specific function and value in religion. The business of doctrine is to achieve that.

Distinctions between the different "languages of faith" are never black and white. There are doctrines in the New Testament. And even the most dry-as-dust doctrinal statements make some appeal to piety or prayer. Still, in spite of the overlap, it is important to keep clear the different functions of the several sources of catechesis; especially when we are planning for religious education or constructing a curriculum.

What is Doctrine For?

143. What does doctrine do in the life of the whole Church and of the individual Christian?

First of all, doctrinal agreement plays an important part in achieving and maintaining the unity of the Church. It is not what actually holds the Church together. The body of Christ is truly held together by him alone and not by human words and ideas. Nonetheless, the Church is a human organisation as well. That human organisation must reflect the invisible reality which it also is; must reflect its unity as well as its other qualities. Unity in a human organisation depends among other things, on common statements of belief; and these beliefs must be expressed in a clear and comprehensive way. You could not speak sensibly of unity in a mixed group of flat-earthers and round-earthers; nor between anarchists and liberal democrats. The Catholic tradition, moreover, contains a strong element of authority. It believes that the gospel of God is in the hands of the teachers of the Church. It is their responsibility to keep it true along the tortuous paths of history. This does not mean that our statements of belief become petrified into one permanent, unchangeable form. It does mean that their development, though continuous, is guided by a teaching authority which cannot fundamentally fail. This authority can only take hold of elements which are external and common. It cannot control our inner experience, our prayer, or the quality of our relationships. It can control doctrinal statements, moral principles and liturgical practice. Hence the importance attached to professions of belief like the creeds, which we say together.

We have seen that doctrine develops, that faith continuously seeks understanding. Consequently, the teaching Church's control over doctrine should not be and usually is not too rigorous. There have been times when heresy-hunters ferreted around, looking for doctrinal error under every bush and tree as though that were the only thing that counted in life. One effect of this is that uniformity is often mistaken for unity, external correctness for inner truth. But our acceptance of doctrinal statements is only of value if it reflects an inner grasp of them. Otherwise we are just conformists. Moreover, heresy-hunting impedes the quest for truth which should constantly go on in the Church. We know that by definition, we can never achieve an exact and perfect statement of the mysteries of our faith.

They are a word that lies beyond human words. Nonetheless, we have to try to give a reasoned account of our faith more clearly and more forcefully, as times change, as knowledge grows, as ideas develop. Theologians, whose business this is, work within the teaching authority of the Church. They must have reasonable freedom to think, to publish their ideas and to engage in argument. Otherwise we shall never get ahead. The speculations of theologians are not Catholic doctrine. But they are a sign and a reminder that the Church's doctrines are, on the one hand true and on the other, never exhaustive or final. We live in a tradition where identity and change co-exist. Education in doctrine is to help people to get inside that tradition.

Doctrine, then, is one important factor in ensuring and promoting the unity of the Church. But it also plays an important part in the Church's mission. Showing the reason for the hope that is within us, is one way (by no means the only one) in which people come to accept with their minds, as well as their feelings, God's saving grace. This "reason for our hope" is not only the "apologetics" which has a long history in our Church; that is, offering external, philosophical reasons to support belief in God and his revelation. It is also the casting of the mysteries of our faith into forms which show their rationality and their inner coherence; and which, for that reason, promote conviction. One aspect of the Church's preaching of her gospel is simply "repent and believe". Another is "find meaning". Neither can go it alone.

144. What place has doctrine in the personal life of a Christian? First of all, it fulfils a natural need to understand and to express — even to ourselves — as clearly as may be, the beliefs and values on which we base our lives. When Plato wrote, "the unexamined life is not liveable by man", perhaps he was being too optimistic. Plenty of people seem to live unreflective lives. Yet there is a need to express our faith in clear ideas which are strong enough to stand up and be counted. It shows itself at certain times of life. It is quite common, for example, among some adolescents who are at a stage where they question the world order and established ideas. It is to be found sometimes at the time of marriage or at some other turning-point which brings the whole basis of life in question. It is, or should be, more common in times like ours, times of rapid change and widespread questioning.

When times are stable and a common faith unquestioned there is no pressure on most people to express their faith clearly to themselves in words and ideas. But when many different faiths are on offer it becomes more important to express a faith clearly. It must be thought out, its reasons personally reflected on, if it is to thrive. Maybe pluralism of belief and the secularisation of society do sometimes lead to lack of interest or cynicism about religious truths. But it is the business of education — one of its purposes — to make people more reflective, knowledgeable and thoughtful about these along with other questions.

So, doctrinal understanding makes a Christian's faith more secure. When we have it, we know that our faith is not a matter of fantasy or feeling; nor does it rest on blind choice, however generous. It has sounder roots. It has more secure foundations. Doctrine also brings an element of maturity to faith — only one element; there are of course other things. But a more know-ledgeable and thoughtful faith can discriminate between what is central and permanent, and what is marginal and likely to change. Doctrinal understanding brings a shape and order to faith. It makes us able to invest our spiritual capital where it really counts, there where rust and moth consumeth not; to avoid putting it where time or history or the vagaries of personal life will erode it away.

Finally — and this may seem an odd claim — doctrinal understanding promotes tolerance. We may readily connect the word "doctrine" with the word "indoctrination". But the two ideas are in fact very different. What prevents growth, what ferments conflict, what feeds hatred, is the blind and unexamined belief. When we have formulated our faith we have got into the order of reason and dialogue. We are then able to understand the beliefs of others, to appreciate them critically and to sym-pathise with them. This situation is the opposite of relativism and the opposite of doctrinaire prejudice. It is a weak and insecure belief that sets people against each other. A strong well thought-out faith brings people closer together.

We might sum this up by speaking of doctrine as "religious literacy". Illiterate people may have a rich experience, may live satisfying, even heroic lives. But they do not easily learn from, or communicate with, those who do not belong to their world. Literacy, by opening up the road to understanding, widens im-measurably the human horizons.

In the same way, a doctrinal grasp of faith, truly achieved, enriches, broadens and deepens that faith.

145. The two are often set against each other, always to the disadvantage of doctrine. It is said to be dry, abstract and dull, whereas experience is warm, immediate and attractive. There is some truth in this but we must not exaggerate it. Doctrine is, by its nature, a "second-order" affair. It inevitably stands back a little from the grinding edge of life. But reading and counting are also second-order skills and we do not consider them unimportant. Nor should we separate them too rigidly from "experience" in its more obvious sense. Look at the excitement of the child for whom the black squiggles on the page suddenly come into focus; who suddenly discovers that they are meaningful, the door into a new world. Doctrinal understanding, when it rings true, is an experience, even though it stands at one remove from the experience of conversion or a moment of grace. It can of course get too remote from experience. It can become no more than a set of rather dull concepts. But a good teacher will prevent this from happening.

Moreover, doctrine can deepen or even create experience. A grasp of the doctrine of the Holy Eucharist, for example, is far more to us than an interesting piece of knowledge. It makes a difference, perhaps all the difference, to the way we share in that sacrament. We should not, I think, make too black-and-white a distinction. Doctrinal understanding need not be doctrinaire, nor need it be a collection of mental fossils. But it will only thrive on experience of religious life and the two must stay close to each other.

What does "learning a doctrine" mean?

146. There are different kinds of learning. We can learn facts or simple skills like riding a bicycle. We can learn to think critically or creatively. There is a kind of learning which touches attitudes and feelings. There is a blind parrot-like learning of nonsense-syllables or formulas. There is insightful learning which involves perceiving patterns and principles. The learning which is possible also varies according to age and intelligence. Learning has to be well-motivated, it is closely connected with interest. In the light of all this complexity and variety, what general account can we give of learning a doctrine?

We can pick out four factors which should characterise good doctrinal learning.

(a) *Insight and Understanding*

147. Doctrine especially should be taught in a way which leads to understanding. For a grasp of the content of faith with the mind is one of the purposes of catechesis. So explanation of doctrine should be, so far as possible, adapted to the stage of development which children have reached. This principle cannot be applied too rigidly. If we waited for mature understanding we should wait a long time. The classical expressions of faith, such as the Creeds, should be learned before they can be fully understood; like the Church's great prayers. But catechists should aim at making these formulas as well understood as possible.

Since doctrine consists of concepts and ideas, learning them with understanding requires a grasp of these concepts; just as learning mathematics demands a grasp of ideas like area and shape, as well as the ability to compute. Some of the concepts used in our doctrines are very abstract — they speak of humanity and godhead, of substance and person. At what age is it possible to understand these ideas as opposed to learning the words? Some people say that they are beyond the grasp of anyone except sophisticated adults. It is true that their abstractness presents some problems. But in the next section we will present a more hopeful view.

(b) *Coherence*

148.   Things are learned well if they are connected with what we know already and if they form meaningful patterns in our minds. Doctrine well-taught and well-learned should at all costs avoid being a random jumble. It should have shape and order, inner unity and coherence. This involves observing carefully what *The General Catechetical Directory* calls "the hierarchy of truths". A good doctrinal presentation is one in which central things are seen to be central and marginal things marginal. This coherent sweep, the architecture of christian truths, does more than improve understanding. It moves doctrinal knowledge a step nearer to faith itself. For it offers a total vision of life which demands a personal response as well as a mental grasp.

(c) *A Sense of Development*

149.   We mean by this that good doctrinal learning should include some awareness that doctrine has grown up over the years. It should not leave the impression of having got hold of something static, fixed and final. We should not, having learned it, feel that we have come to the end of the road of understanding. To say this is not to encourage relativism.

We do not mean that the learner should think of doctrine as provisional or not properly true; only that he should not think of it as final or exhaustive. Doctrine has a geography which we expressed in the word "coherence". We should have a sense of that geography. It also has a history and we should have an awareness of that too. There is a doctrinal tradition which is alive and therefore still developing. We are in that tradition.

(d) *Relevance*

150. It is sometimes said that doctrine is abstract, remote and not relevant to life. This can happen. It can degenerate into the clever manipulation of words and ideas or into a mere façade of orthodox formulas. But it need not happen. It is possible to teach the doctrine of the Trinity in such a way that it throws a great deal of light on the character of human relationships. The doctrine of the Eucharist both illuminates and questions the nature of human communities. Doctrine will be neither interesting nor valuable if it stands away from life. A teacher should be constantly looking for ways of making links, connections and applications.

151. We might take as an instance the central doctrine of the Incarnation. It can be comprehensible if some grasp of the ideas of "nature" and "person" can be achieved. This need not be very abstract. They can be presented concretely with plenty of examples. The doctrine can be made coherent if it is seen in the context of the question: Why did God become man? It should be of a piece with the whole history of salvation; related to man's fallen condition, to redemption, to our hopes for the future. How can a sense of development grow? It will come from some knowledge of the scriptural origins of the doctrine and of how it was argued out during the turmoils of the fourth century. Students should come to see that Peter's words, "Master, to whom should we go?" already express total faith in Christ.

What the Church is doing over the next centuries is trying to work out, in ideas and propositions, who and what Christ is, that He should be our only source of hope. Finally, the doctrine should be relevant in that it should offer a transforming vision of life; the essential goodness of our world, of human life and of secular reality; and a sense of confidence in life which is backed up by substantial belief and is not mere euphoria.

Can doctrine be put simply?

152. Jerome Bruner wrote, "anything can be taught to any child at any age in a way that is intellectually honest, provided it is sufficiently well thought through". Perhaps this is rather idealistic. Maybe there are ideas which simply are in themselves too difficult. But the important thing in the principle is that you can "think through" an idea or system at many different levels, from the most abstract to the most concrete. You can do this in a way which does not simplify the idea out of existence. What matters is to get hold of the key-concepts and ways of thinking and to embody these in different forms. So there is no reason in principle why a doctrine or a whole doctrinal system should not be presented in a concrete way. It demands close co-operation between theologians and educators.

Direct and Thematic Teaching

153. Nothing that has been said so far necessarily implies that doctrine should be taught directly. It is common nowadays to teach religion through themes from human experience, like friendship, suffering or justice. The idea is that doctrines can be embodied in these themes. It is a more interesting way of teaching which follows the principle, "start from where the children are". Doctrines can be learned incidentally and painlessly. There is certainly a good deal of truth in this and a good deal of value in this way of teaching.

It is also open to certain criticisms. One is that what we think is going to happen incidentally sometimes gets lost on the way. Some hoped that grammar and spelling might be learned through talking and creative writing. But this did not always happen. There are some structures in language (a few modest, realistic, basic ones) which can be, and ought to be, taught formally and directly (which does not mean abstractly or mechanically). Similarly there is room for doctrinal themes as well as life themes in religious teaching, provided that they are well thought-out. But the main point is that *however* it is taught, directly or thematically, there are some principles which should be observed. One of the things that should guide any doctrinal teaching is the true nature and function of doctrine itself. A proper grasp of that will ensure that it finds its true place in the curriculum.

How Necessary is Doctrine?

154. Certainly no great amount or depths of doctrinal knowledge is essential for true faith. The early Church had very few doctrinal formulas. Many Christians and some saints have had, and have, a very sketchy doctrinal understanding. Mentally handicapped people sometimes cannot form concepts at all. The whole doctrinal dimension of their faith is missing. Yet no one can doubt that they have a true religious life which expresses itself in other ways. Nevertheless, for those who have the ability, growth in understanding of their faith is both a duty and a necessity. For understanding of the faith brings it to greater maturity. Doctrine may seem a plain and humble handmaid of faith. But the tasks she does are very necessary ones.

A fresh look at doctrinal teaching is not going to work any miracles. What we have been saying here implies very little directly about syllabus or method: though we believe that in thematic teaching, themes which have a doctrinal basis and structure should complement those which begin from experience. Again, the questions of age, intelligence and social background are wholly separate questions which must affect syllabus and method in important ways. But there are two conclusions which we stand by. The first is that religious teaching which does not absorb the richness of the Church's doctrine is bound to be impoverished and thin. The second is that whenever and however doctrine is taught, there are certain principles which define its function and govern its communication.

3 — Liturgy and Learning

155. We have said that the true content of catechesis is the mysteries of our faith. The four "content areas" we are discussing now are four bodies of material through which those mysteries may be reached. At the beginning of Mass we speak of the Eucharist as "the sacred mysteries". After the Consecration we "proclaim the mystery of faith". The use of these phrases suggests that the connection of the liturgy with those mysteries is closer than that of doctrine or of life-experience. Its place in religious education is a very important one. In some way it enables us to share in those mysteries more comprehensively and deeply. It is also the most direct and powerful way in which those mysteries form Christians in their faith.

Because it is so close to the mysteries of the faith themselves, liturgy resists analysis more than the rest of the "four ways" do. Doctrine is faith teased out into ideas and concepts. The study of scripture yields literary forms and facts. The mystery of faith in liturgy is much more an indivisible totality in which christian truths are not so much expressed as embodied or embedded. The old proverb, "lex orandi, lex credendi", "the law of praying is the law of believing" does not mean just that liturgy is a prayerful way of expressing doctrines which are already believed. No, liturgy stands on its own feet. It is a language of faith of importance equal to if not greater than that of doctrinal formulas. This does not mean that we can say nothing about it.

There are several important and complementary principles which must be stated. It does mean that, as with scriptures or doctrine, the place of liturgy in catechesis must follow its nature and function. It must reflect its essential character and its place in christian life.

156. The first principle is that education in liturgy is what it says. It is not reducing liturgy to clear and distinct ideas, the way you might explain how a refrigerator works or the procedure of the County Council. It is certainly not a matter of giving a little sermon every few minutes to explain what's happening in case people should miss something. There is a real temptation to over-explaining. The danger of this is that it reduces the liturgy to something else. Then the liturgy loses its power to be itself and to do its own work.

Although we are mostly happy to have the liturgy in our own language, we should take note of the danger which that change brought in its train. It is the tendency to wordiness; the danger of reducing the Word to words. There is a "liturgy of the word". But liturgy is at work in other media too. It is visual and active, it is colour and gesture, movement and music, sign, symbol and celebration. We ought not to think that learning through the liturgy is only of the kind that can be measured by tests. It has its own being, its own special character and its place in catechesis must follow from that. We shall set out shortly some of the elements which will shape that place.

157. To say that, however, is not to say that liturgy stands entirely on its own. It has to be prepared for. That preparation requires some measure of explanation and understanding. So any attempt to make the liturgy live inevitably draws some educational process in its wake. Sometimes the catechesis involved is of crucial importance, sometimes built into the liturgy itself — for instance through the scrutinies in the baptism of adults. There are in life, times of great potential, times especially favourable to deep and effective catechesis, for example the birth of a child, first Communion, marriage, the time of death. These times are usually marked by some especially solemn liturgy. Preparation for these liturgies which give pattern and shape to life are not an extra bonus. They are a major part of the substance of catechesis through liturgy. In addition to them, there is the preparation for more everyday liturgical events: house Masses, classroom Masses, the sacrament of reconciliation. It adds up to a substantial and important body of catechesis through liturgy. Our point here is that liturgy must not become top-heavy with theory and explanation. There are other forms of preparation as well as lessons.

158. We must also recall that liturgy is primarily the worship of God and the enactment of the Lord's redeeming work towards us. It is not in the first place a tool for religious education. We must get this priority right, otherwise liturgy will become distorted from the true. Worship of God is a right and duty and necessity for children and simple people as well as for those who are educated and formed in the faith. If catechesis follows that principle it will find its proper level and character and will not become something contrived and artificial.

Elements in Liturgy

Mystery and the Sacred

159. Liturgy has to do with God. It should always contain something of that spirit which impelled Moses to loose the shoes from his feet when he stood on holy ground. It should always include the feeling of awe which issues in the act of worship. It is true that, because of our belief in the Incarnation, christian worship more readily embodies itself in ordinary human acts and signs. Our dealings with God are always mediated through the work of the Lord, both in his historical life and in his continued life in the Church and in the world. Nevertheless, the dazzle of eternal light — the spirit of the Transfiguration, "Lord, it is good for us to be here", should always be present. Perhaps this feeling of the transcendent among us is now much more evident in eastern liturgies than in our own, which has grown recently much more domestic and familiar. We should make sure that it is not lost. Many believe that children have a natural sense of awe and wonder which the empirical humanism, the systems and structures of our world quickly wear away. It is not the business of liturgical education to accelerate this process. On the contrary, it should nourish and develop in them a sense of reverence for holy things, a feeling of awe in the face of the mystery of the Universe, and its Lord. It should keep this sense alive in all of us; along with the recognition that our faith has to do with mysteries and must not get reduced in our minds to doctrinal beliefs, moral rules or ritual practices.

160. Although our liturgy is in one sense given from above, in another sense it arises from among us, from our experience and from our human tasks. It is built up out of things we see and hear, out of needs, ideas and images we have in our minds. It is in one sense the acts of God, in another our own expressions. In the same way, the person of Jesus was divine. His humanity was built up from the flesh of Mary and from the culture and customs of Israel. The Holy Eucharist we believe to be both the sacrifice of Christ made present sacramentally and our own offering of ourselves to God. Liturgy is about both where we are in God's sight and in his love and also where we are at the moment in ourselves. It should make both of these aspects visible.

161. Many of the things we use in liturgy — water, oil, bread, the gestures of bowing and lifting our hands — have a connection with living our human lives which is deep and ancient. In the case of some of our symbols, it belongs to a remote period of history; some may even be unconscious and timeless. Other things that we use or say are recent attempts to make a direct and evident connection between life-experience and worship. Examples of this are, at Mass, offertory processions and the sign of peace and bidding prayers.

The same tendency can be seen at work in such renewed and reconstructed liturgies as the rite of reconciliation and the anointing of the sick. In catechesis we ought to use both these ways of realising the humanity of the liturgy. In the first place we should try to revive sensitivity to the ancient symbols at a time when they seem to have lost their hold on the minds of many people. We speak of "sensitivity" to symbols and this word should serve as a sufficient warning that "learning a symbol" is not the same as "knowing what it means". Over-explaining symbols can destroy their true function and make them useless in the liturgy. Equally, we ought to be able to adapt the liturgy in such a way that familiar things are taken up into its movement and nature. They must be "taken up" or assimilated, for liturgy is not just a human construct. Familiar elements should be built into liturgy in such a way that they appear differently and our feelings about them are changed. This is one of the most difficult as well as the most important areas of liturgical catechesis. The celebrant or the teacher must be able to manage it so that liturgy neither becomes too remote nor loses its quality of mystery and the sacred.

Patterns, Seasons and the Paschal Mystery

162. Human life must have a pattern. Otherwise it is scarcely liveable. It lapses into meaninglessness, a state which is common today and which is the source of much unhappiness. This pattern stands outside the ebb and flow of ordinary everyday affairs, the things we feel or choose to do or that happen to us, the way we grow or decay. It is a structure or a set of structures which give shape, order and meaning to all human living. Without it, human beings become confused and helpless. It is true that pattern or meaning can be provided by ideas, beliefs or values; which we can hold in our heads in a way that makes experience meaningful.

Yet what we have in our heads is not what we live by. Moreover, we are social beings who live in community. The meaning of life is only rarely an individual matter. Most often it is something that people share with each other and learn from the community in which they live. So life is patterned by events, rituals and celebrations which are not purely mental and which are in some way part of public life. Primitive life was highly patterned; elaborate ceremonies marked all the important events of personal and tribal life. The core of these was called the "rites of passage". They were the ceremonies that marked birth, the beginning of adult life, marriage and death. With great power they expressed and taught the beliefs of the community about the meaning and value of these events.

In modern life only a few relics of the rites of passage remain. Indeed the whole idea that the meaning of life should be celebrated and communicated by rituals has largely disappeared. Yet the underlying realities remain and the need for meaning remains. The sacraments are among other things our "rites of passage". They present and teach a map of life, the route which faith takes through it, the meaning it gives to it. They teach the faith in a way which is not purely mental, but active, appealing to feeling and a deep human need. Hence the importance of working to make the sacraments live; also the importance of the catechesis which is connected with them.

We need to grasp and feel the meaning not only of life as a whole, but also of each year, season and day. The liturgy not only marks out the main lines of life. It also, through its yearly cycle of seasons and through the great feasts, gives pattern to the more humdrum cycles of our life. The turning seasons — seed-time to harvest, midwinter to the summer solstice, mingle with the cycles of the mysteries of the Lord's life. The centre of this yearly cycle is the paschal mystery. This is a complex and rich idea. It is enough to say here that we share in the expectation of our Lord, his coming to earth, his work, his death, resurrection and return to the Father. Joining ourselves into the movement of these events means more than recalling them in a dramatic way. It means that these events of passing through life and death to the Father is re-enacted in our own lives. It is the work of grace within us. This yearly "living through" of the liturgy is itself an important catechesis: one which affects attitudes and feeling perhaps more than increasing knowledge.

It also requires understanding in celebrant and teacher; preparation and commentary which can go beyond explanation and can involve the arts and drama.

163. We have already noted that liturgy more than the other content-areas, defies analysis. It is relatively simple to map out what happens when we learn a fact like the date of the Battle of Hastings; or a concept like that of area; or a skill like that of typing. But clearly, liturgy, by its very nature, works through attitudes, feelings and relationships. It is much harder to be precise about it. Perhaps we should not use the word "education" which nowadays has a technical meaning, but speak of catechesis or of formation. Liturgy forms those who come to it in faith. Others may enjoy it as one enjoys music, but that is something different.

When we say "liturgy acts through attitudes and feelings" we have already begun to analyse it. For it is the total human person who shares in liturgy and is formed by it. Nevertheless, if we are to see how to use liturgy in catechesis, some breaking down must be done. We must know what happens or should happen in human beings who share in the liturgy if we are to exploit its possibilities. In the following section we pick out those aspects of liturgy which are particularly important in catechesis.

Language

164. A great part of liturgy consists of speech; readings, prayers, blessings, dialogues. When our liturgy was in Latin, this presented no problem. The assumption was that usually the words of the liturgy would not be understood except perhaps at second-hand by those who followed a translation. So the style and presentation of the words was not a question. In a vernacular liturgy it is. Vernacular speech is meant to be understood or at least to affect the hearers in some way. So the choice of words, phrasing, imagery, rhythm and the oral presentation of texts become important questions.

They do not, strictly speaking, fall within the scope of religious education. Liturgists are the ones who construct liturgical texts. Still, for two reasons they concern us indirectly.

First, those concerned with religious education have to collaborate with liturgists, especially where children's liturgies are concerned. Secondly, although in general the text to be used is laid down, some room is left for adaptation and spontaneity. For example, the homily and the bidding prayers are both part of the liturgy. In liturgies for children there is much scope for adaptation (cf. the *Directory on Children's Masses*, nn. 23, 47, 50, 51). We should then face two questions concerning language and liturgy.

First, we should consider how to educate children to respond to liturgical speech. Secondly, we should set out some principles to guide us when we have to use our own words in liturgy.

The first question need not detain us long. The principles laid down earlier about scripture apply here. It is possible to learn a special technical language. This does not only mean explaining the meaning of words and phrases. For it is not only with mental understanding that we are concerned. It is necessary also to learn to respond to the poetic as well as the prose meaning of words, to their associations and movement as well as their connotation. Visual and musical experience, mime and drama can often enrich the meaning of words in this way. The general principles of the teaching and learning of language apply here.

Secondly, how should we set about constructing liturgical texts where this is allowed? This is an important matter when we remember the substantial body of research which shows how the actual style of language affects both intellectual and emotional development in children. The language must be comprehensible and simple on the one hand, familiar and related to daily experience on the other.

Again, we must recall that mental understanding is not everything. Liturgical language can be beyond the mental grasp of children yet can affect them in other ways. Moreover, although liturgy is in one sense built up out of daily life, it is also concerned with the mystery of God. It should lift ordinary human words out of their everyday context. An excess of familiarity, the use of slang or careless, sloppy language, can destroy this element in liturgy. We should look for a language which is clear and familiar but which yet has about it some beauty and dignity. There are a number of books (collections of bidding prayers, children's penance services, etc.) which offer models.

Symbols and Signs

165. We are familiar with the idea of sacrament as an "outward sign of inward grace", a sign which makes present the reality which it signifies. Signs and symbols are realities which both are present to the sense and recall some reality which is not present and sometimes cannot ever be. Some symbols are superficial, like the constructed symbols in industry which are rallying-points and reminders of a firm or business. Symbols used in the liturgy go deeper. They are concerned, as all religion is, with realities at the heart of human life. They form part of the sacraments, but are widely used throughout liturgical actions; lighted candles, incense, holy water, bread and wine. Symbols

G

do not stand for one idea, the way many words correspond to only one meaning. They stand for a mysterious reality which cannot be made present in any other way. So they cannot be explained as you might explain the meaning of a word, or a theorem in geometry. They are full of meaning, but it is a meaning we can only enter into indirectly.

Some people have thought symbols so important that they defined man as a "symbol-making animal". Some even believe that there are symbols so deeply rooted in human nature that they crop up in all cultures, societies and religions. On the other hand, some think that symbols are the specific product of a culture or a kind of culture. So, when a particular society collapses, the symbols it used lose their meaning. Hence, some people argue that the liturgical symbols we use are mostly products of a nomadic, agricultural society. They think that most people today who live in a technological, man-made world cannot respond to them. They think that we are too far removed from the source of life. Bread comes to us baked and sliced, and wine from some remote part of the world, oil goes into engines, and water comes without difficulty from reservoirs. So these elemental symbols touch no chord in us.

No doubt the scientific humanist character of our times does make symbols less effective. We do live largely in a man-made world. Still we cannot say that the need to use symbols has vanished. For some young people a motor-cycle is the symbol of a whole way of life; and we have already noticed the use of symbols in industry and commerce. It may be that liturgy can be adapted by introducing new symbols into it. Nevertheless, there are some symbols which are a permanent and essential part of our sacramental system; for instance, bread and wine, oil and water.

So the problem arises: How can we help people in these times to respond to christian symbol? Even from a purely educational point of view it is not an unreasonable thing to attempt. For education should, among other things, aim to liberate people from the dominance of what is in the vivid foreground of their immediate world.

It is important to recall that it is not a question of explaining what symbols mean. If they are reduced to some purely logical meaning, they cease to be symbols. It is a question of developing a sensitivity rather than a rational understanding. We look therefore to those ways of teaching which aim to encourage sensitivity; chiefly to the way in which the arts are taught. It is true that the experience which made symbols so vividly effective in some cultures is rarely available at first hand. But it can be offered at second hand. Projects, visual presentations, literature, drama, can in their different ways fill out for contemporary men and women the lost meaning of ancient symbols. They can create responses, heighten or alter feelings. This is a difficult kind of teaching. It is easy to lose your way completely and results cannot be measured as they might be if knowledge was the object. Yet liturgy cannot teach unless worshippers become able to respond to the symbols which form so important a part of it.

Celebration and the Education of Feelings

166.   It is a great, though common mistake to think that religious education is concerned only with knowledge and mental understanding. It is probably true that education in the West has for a very long time been dominated by knowledge and rational abilities; that the education of the emotions has been neglected. Some people might even say that "educating" the emotions is a contradiction in terms. Yet feeling plays an important part in religious life, in faith, in devotion, in morality. When we are analysing and trying to justify the different elements in the content of religious education, we cannot neglect those elements which are directed largely towards emotional development. In the world of education recently there has been a considerable revival of interest in the education of emotion. This is both encouraging and helpful.

What is it to educate emotions? First there are two mistaken but common views which must be ruled out. The first of these is the idea that to educate feeling is to suppress it.

This is an outlook which the Victorian public school tradition and the English stiff upper lip typify. In the life of our Church probably Jansenism, excessively rational scholasticism, perhaps even the Manichees have left some traces. These crop up in an attitude never openly stated but sometimes implied, that feeling is bad or at least suspect. Of course we have to act against our emotions sometimes. But then we also have to act against our pride which springs from the mind and the will. It is well known that the blind suppression of emotion often has very harmful consequences. Acting against emotions should be done in full awareness and acceptance of them. We do no service to children if we try to teach them simply to suppress their feelings or just to walk away from them.

The other mistaken view is that we ought to whip up feelings into a state of excitement. There are approaches in religious education (some of those which put the emphasis on creating religious experience) which attempt to do this. We sympathise with the desire to offer real religious experience to others. But religious teaching which relies too much on arousing feeling often has very shortlived results.

What then does it mean "to educate the emotions"? It means learning to direct emotions to appropriate targets. Most feelings are directed towards something that really exists. If you meet an armed band of thugs you feel fear, and rightly so. The thugs are an appropriate, a perfectly rational target for fear. They may well rob you or even kill you. But some people are afraid of things which give no reasonable ground for fear, like crowds or open spaces. To educate emotion is to lead the feelings towards objects which are reasonable and right.

Some emotions are particularly important in religious life; for example feelings of awe and reverence which lead to worship, feelings of gratitude which lead to thanksgiving, feelings of guilt which lead to repentance. One purpose of religious education is to direct these feelings towards their proper targets. Liturgy involves "celebration". It is therefore more directly concerned with feelings. Because it involves listening and praying, song, symbol and ceremony, it has a more direct emotional impact than say, doctrine does. One of its functions (not the only one) is to provide a structure for those feelings and lead them precisely where they ought to be.

Let us take one example. The new rite of Penance is intended to restore that sacrament to a fuller place in the Church's liturgy.

It also has the purpose of educating Christians towards a truer sense of sin. We have (rightly) feelings of guilt about our sins. But frequently these feelings are misdirected. They may be directed solely to the breaking of moral rules. In this case our guilt stops short at crime and does not reach its proper target of sin. They may be directed solely to external actions without taking any account of motive and intention. In this case we may feel unreasonably guilty about things we are not responsible for. The liturgy of penance is aimed at directing these feelings of guilt at their proper target; that is, at sins as damage to our relationship with God. The readings, hymns, prayers, the examination of conscience and the act of repentance form a channel in which feelings flow towards their true goal. In a similar way, the Eucharist is a channel for feelings of awe and thanksgiving, the Easter Vigil directs feelings of joy to their proper target in faith, the resurrection of Christ.

So the liturgy is a powerful way of educating these feelings which are important in religion. It is not a question for the celebrant or participants, of putting feeling into liturgical texts or ceremonies, or presenting these in an emotional way. They have their own power. What is important is to realise the texts, ceremonies and symbols so that they can carry the feelings along as they are meant to. This requires an understanding of the structure, meaning, themes and movements of our liturgies.

Participation

167.   Before the liturgical renewal, most people's part in the liturgy was mainly a passive one. It was thought that the laity's part should be inner union with what was actively done by the priest. Of course, the idea of inner sharing remains the most important form of participation. Nevertheless, a more active physical participation is necessary if liturgical life is to thrive. One reason for this is that liturgy is not like private prayer. It is the public, corporate act of God's people. Therefore we join in it, not only by a kind of inner meditation, but also by an outer, active sharing. The Church's worship follows the principle on Incarnation. It is done "in the flesh".

A second reason concerns the power of the liturgy to form and educate Christians. We know that, other things being equal, learning improves when the learner is active in the process. A lesson which involves questions and discussion is more than one which is simply listened to. Things we find out for ourselves are remembered better than things we are told. So when we participate actively in liturgy, the truths it embodies come home to us. The feelings and attitudes which it involves are actively channelled to their goal.

Active participation in liturgy does not come naturally. It has to be learnt. It is important that, at as early an age as possible, children should be taught how to make responses and bidding prayers; should learn hymns, how to give the sign of peace and join an offertory procession and how to prepare the altar. These celebrations of the Eucharist which are most closely connected with education — Mass for classes or family groups at home — are the ones which offer most scope for active participation.

Community

168.   Active participation — things said and done together — is closely linked with the idea of community which is so strong an emphasis in liturgical life today. Liturgy should both express the shared life of community which already exists and also build up a sense of community among worshippers. Sometimes it is true, participants have no other connection with each other, beyond the fact of being at Mass together. In this case it is very difficult to build up any sense of community. However, the case of a class at school, of a family group, of a neighbourhood is different. Here there is a considerable area of shared life. Here the relationship between liturgy and community becomes practicable and important. Many educators believe that the absence of shared celebrations impoverishes the life and the growth of children today. Feelings of fellowship and belonging do not develop; nor does the awareness of shared values and beliefs which is so important in handing on the faith. In Church schools and other educational groups, liturgy should fill this gap.

How does community develop through the liturgy? Chiefly in two ways. First there is the effect of united attention to God. This provides a focal point. When awareness of attention to a common Father is real, the idea of a family extends itself to all who worship together. For this reason, it is a mistake to try to make liturgy too "horizontal"; to envisage it as largely interaction among the members of the group. A sense of community does not grow only because the members of a group relate to each other well. It requires also a common goal and shared beliefs which lie outside the group to which, corporately, it directs its attention. It is also necessary that the unity created by this expresses itself openly in liturgical ways; for example through bidding prayers and the sign of peace.

Secondly, besides being directed to a common point, the group also expresses the same truths, hopes and attitudes. It is true that individually, many members may not have much personal grasp on these. Inevitably because they "collect" the prayers of individual believers into the common prayer of the Church, liturgical texts have a certain impersonality about them. Nevertheless to join in the liturgy has the effect of creating those attitudes common to the whole Church as well as expressing them. Gradually, if he is given the right kind of help (for instance in preparing liturgies or in homilies) the liturgy begins to shape a worshipper's mind and feelings.

The creation of a sense of community is extremely important; not only because it is a good in itself. It is perhaps the main way in which a sense of belonging to the Church develops. This goes beyond the sense of being a member of a worshipping community. It extends to awareness of a community of faith, a source of truth, a community of moral wisdom. So it is important for education in the areas of doctrine and morality. It is not for nothing that we recite the Creed together in the liturgy; not for nothing that it contains so many calls and dedications to christian moral life. Beliefs, moral commitments and feelings are the main components of attitudes. Liturgy touches and shapes attitudes more directly than any other content area.

Adaptation

169. The texts and ceremonies of the liturgy are built up, translated or approved by the Church. But nowadays, some room is left for adaptation; as the *Directory on Children's Masses* makes clear. Within the limits set, liturgy may be adapted to an occasion, for instance a pilgrimage or a national celebration. Or it may be adapted to the needs and mentality of those taking part, for instance, children or handicapped people.

Here a delicate balance must be kept. Liturgy is not our own to do as we like with. It belongs to the whole people of God, and goes beyond our immediate interests and needs. The external uniformity of words and gestures expresses this. Moreover, it is a mistake to think that liturgy should be adapted so that everything in it can be understood. This is another example of the error we spoke of earlier, the error of translating liturgy into a lesson. The texts need not be fully understood. The symbols and ceremonies cannot be fully understood. The mysteries of faith go beyond prose meanings. Our effort should be to help others to enter into the whole movement of the liturgy.

On the other hand, the liturgy must be able to speak. It does contain lessons. It does depend to some extent, on understanding meanings in the ordinary way. It must communicate. Hence the need to be able to adapt some of the words for groups who would not understand the regular forms. For example, the *Directory on Children's Masses* speaks of the celebrant using his own words at the invitation to the penitential rite, to the Lord's prayer, to the sign of peace. These words can be less formal than usual. The aim is to establish a more direct relationship with children, to speak in words familiar to them. Priests are sometimes not able to do this very well. They should consult those who are class teachers or parents.

Children's Liturgy

170. The idea that liturgy should be adapted for children is relatively new. It should be approached with care. Sometimes adaptation seems to produce only what adults believe children think and feel, not what they really do. Moreover the way in which our culture looks at childhood has its limitations. The "child-centred" approach which has been commonly accepted over the last century or so, has led to some strange aberrations.

Again the liturgy is basically unitive. In Christ there is neither

Jew nor Greek, male nor female, slave nor free. We should be cautious therefore about dividing up those who belong to Christ even into adults and children.

On the other hand our present liturgy is very difficult for children. They cannot always achieve even the limited degree of understanding necessary for real participation in it.

Special liturgies for children should emphasise educational aspects. Many of those, along with many of the problems of understanding are concentrated into the liturgy of the word. So the practice of separated adapted liturgy of the word for children has a lot to commend it.

Finally the Eucharist is not the whole of the liturgy. There are other sacraments. Beyond that, there are sacramentals and other ceremonies. Liturgies such as the Rite for the *Christian Initiation of Adults,* attempt to recapture some of the richness of prayers and gestures which exist in the Church's liturgy. It represents a treasure-house of resources. Moreover, it is possible to find or devise broadly liturgical family ceremonies, especially for Easter and Christmas. They too, apart from their value in themselves, form part of the liturgical component of religious education.

4 — *Experience as Content*

171. The fourth content-area is rather different from the other three; each of those has a definite connection with the mysteries which are the true content of faith. This is not necessarily true of experience. People have the experience of being in love or over-whelmed by beauty, suffering or being afraid, whether they have faith or not. Yet it is certain that faith, if it is to thrive must be of a piece with our experience of life. If it remains in a separate compartment it will not have strong roots. It will ring hollow.

172. Two different words have been used for this fourth content area. In older catechetical writing it is called "witness". The implications of this word is that religious education must be concerned with how the faith is lived as well as how it is under-stood. The way Christians confront the world, their problems, their achievements and the quality of their lives make up a body of content. The history of the Church, the lives of the saints, the problems and successes of the Church as a body and of its indi-vidual members are the way the faith is embodied in the world made visible and credible there.

173. The word "experience" involves a different idea. It is rather vague and ambiguous. Generally it means the total effect on us of events both inside and outside ourselves before this is examined and analysed. On the one hand we have ideas and theories about various aspects of life, on the other the immediate total feel of them. Except to academic people, the latter is more absorbing. When presented to us, it makes a greater impact. Experience catches the interest and stimulates curiosity. Questions follow which lead to theories and formulations. These are learned more easily and with greater understanding. They are more memorable and more permanent. A walk across the hills may lead to interest in the formation of the landscape and bring home the necessity of learning to read maps. A visit to an old building stimulates a curiosity about the lives and doings of people in the remote past. It is easy to see that there is a good deal of truth in this. How does the idea apply to religious education?

174. First of all there is overtly religious experience. To pray, to share in the liturgy, to go on a pilgrimage, may, apart from their value in themselves, lead to vivid learning of many things about God, about the sacraments, about the christian community and its common quest. Certainly we ought to provide occasions for religious experience of this sort. It is not easy to do this in the classroom because of the place or because of the timetable or because of the relationships which sometimes exist in class. Still there are some opportunities: for instance in teaching prayer or in the preparation and celebration of a class Mass. There are other opportunities which lie outside the classroom in the life of the school community; through its liturgy, through extra-curricular activities, social service and works of charity and through the quality of that community's life. There are even more chances in the groups and structures which exist for adult education. None of these chances should be missed. For without some experience of belonging to a real community of faith, it is hard to see how the faith can be grasped and held with any kind of depth or permanence.

175. So far we have spoken of experience arising directly from religious beliefs and acts; how the truths of faith are applied in everyday life; how it feels to pray or to join the community in worship. More often however, experience is thought of differently and is included in the content of religious education on other grounds. These are that some human experiences which have no distinctively religious character have nonetheless an implicit connection with the truths of faith. There are different views about what that connection is. The widespread inclusion of "real-life themes" in religious education is often criticised on the grounds that it reduces religion to humanism. So it is important that we clarify the principle involved here.

176. The first view is that life-experience can provide vivid illustrations of religious truths; or that for those who have no explicit religious faith it can be used to prepare the ground for it. There is no particular difficulty about this view. It is obviously right to illustrate the truths of faith from familiar things, as our Lord did in the parables. There are sometimes groups whose background in the faith is almost non-existent and who seem disinterested, even hostile. Often these are young people whose experience and upbringing has been, humanly speaking, unfavourable or deprived. Their lives so far have left them with little sense of values, little desire to understand life more deeply than in terms of immediate satisfactions.

A teacher may find it best to try to awaken in them some sensitivity to human and social values with the hope that this may create better soil for the reception of the word of the gospel. This idea of a "preparatio evangelii", educational work which tries to develop a sense of values while presenting the faith only in terms of care, kindness and service, is an ancient one. It is valid not only in missionary countries but also among the baptised where faith has had no chance to grow or has been overwhelmed by hostile influences. However, with those who belong to the Church, even in a basic baptismal sense those responsible for pastoral and educational care should not permanently evade speaking the explicit word of faith.

177. There is however another view which maintains that human events and experiences have in themselves a religious character, though an anonymous one. This is said to be true especially of those experiences which in some way uncover the roots and the most important elements in the human condition: our relationships, our freedom, our significant hopes, conflicts and sufferings, the mystery of the human person and human race, our destiny, our purposes, our death. When we think of these things and speak of them we are already moving in the world of religion. For they represent ultimate significance, the broadest and most comprehensive experience and that is what religion is. This view is sometimes translated into theological terms. God, it is said, reveals himself to us, not only in the words of the scriptures, our liturgy and the doctrine of the Church; but also, perhaps more importantly, in our present experience. If we look at this sensitively and in the right way, we have already entered into a revelatory communion with God. So a religious teacher who is able to deal with experience in this way, has no need to explain it through religious words and ideas. He has already arrived at religious dialogue. We must look at this view carefully for it contains some truth, some ambiguity and some error.

178. The truth is that most human beings have not heard or have not accepted the explicit teaching of the faith. Most of them have believed and practised some other religion. Nowadays in the West most people have no very definite religious belief or commitment at all. Yet they are not outside the mercy of God. Their salvation depends on how they live according to their own lights. Certainly in human freedom, in the love and compassion we find in the world, in the quest for truth and a good life, the grace of God is at work in a hidden anonymous way. Those who promote these qualities through education undoubtedly contribute to human salvation. Still we must ask the question whether we can honestly speak of religion in this way; a way that avoids the challenge of faith and the word of God, of worship and commitment. More immediately we must ask whether there is not here a mistaken idea of revelation.

179. Religion is not the same as the ultimate salvation of mankind. If words are to have any meaning at all it must have a more specific one than that. It means those beliefs and acts which have to do with the existence of a power beyond our human world, and our relationship with that power. Some have justified the view under discussion through the idea of "religionless Christianity". We ought, they argue, to free ourselves from the numerous and complex structures of religious life, the doctrinal formulas, the moral rules, the liturgical forms, the heavy super-structure of Church order. Then we may be able to realise what they think to be the real essence of Christianity, the love of truth, courageous action for justice, the growth of love and goodness in human life. Of course it is true that we can be so bogged down in Church affairs especially if these are many and highly or-ganised, that we miss the wood for the trees. Yet it is true that religion has its own distinctive ways of thinking and acting. These structure the basic human realities which give life; they also mediate to us God's truth and grace. Without them the human qualities and experiences become structureless, even chaotic. Left to themselves, even the best — especially the best — human qualities can run amok and become destructive. The structures of the faith, renewed and alive, give them their true bearings.

180. There is no need to repeat at length, what has been said already, about revelation and religious education. We will only recall that it is true that God speaks to all men in their hearts. Yet the revelation which comes to us in Jesus and is continued in the Church makes plain and open that implicit, anonymous word. So it is that revelation, related to what the mind strives to know and what the heart feels, that provides the main source of the content of explicit religious education. When we discuss these matters, we are not simply arguing about words; as though "religion" and "revelation" were semantic questions of interest only to academic philosophers. No, they are substantial matters. They determine where we shall find the words and ideas on which our religious education will be based. In this way, they determine the future of our Church. Certainly God's saving grace is universal. But the data of revelation, the words and ideas we derive from scripture, doctrine and liturgy, form the explicit expression of that grace which keeps it from going astray. The Church is the first sacrament. This does not only mean that it is the source of the other sacraments which we celebrate in the life of the Church. It also means that the life of the Church community is the explicit expression of God's saving grace as it is found universally and anonymously in the world. Consequently, the sustaining and developing of that life, those words, those ideas, is a responsibility which we have before God not only for ourselves, the christian Church, but also for the whole of our race.

181. These are the principles then which govern the use of experience in religious teaching. It is important that it should be prominent there lest religious faith and truth should seem to be in a compartment separate from the mainstream of life. On the other hand it is not just scaremongering to fear that an extreme concentration on it might reduce religious teaching to a kind of humanism with a vague religious reference. This is the danger to which the "anthropological" or "experience-centred" approach to catechesis is open; an avoidance of specifically religious words and ideas on the grounds that any deep reflection on experience is already religious. How is a good balance to be kept?

182. First of all it is important to say we are speaking here only of religious education in an explicit sense; in school that means religious education as a classroom subject on the time-table; in adult groups, topics which openly declare themselves to be religious — for instance a course on prayer or on the Church or on the sacraments. It is true that other teaching which deals with important human matters may make a valuable contribution to religious education in an implicit or hidden way.

So in a Catholic school there will be an implicit religious element throughout the curriculum. This does not mean that all the subjects are used for vehicles for religious teaching; religion being dragged by the heels into literature or science or history. Subjects are based on particular ways of human understanding. They have their own rights, their own autonomy. It is not honest to try to make them what they are not. On the other hand many subjects have among their goals, self-understanding, a feeling and a love for truth and for its unity, a sense of history and the development of ideas, an awareness of beauty and mystery. These are factors which provide human grounds for the growth of faith. We may even say that they are ways in which God anonymously speaks to us. But religion as a subject, has just like history or physics, its own specific character and this should provide its framework if not the whole of its character.

Human experience as part of the religious lesson

183.   We have already seen that one justification for the use of experience in religious education is the simple fact that religion is about ordinary life as well as about specific beliefs and acts of worship. We have also seen that this contains both a truth and a falsity. It is true that much human experience represents a quest for God or contains implicit religious values. It is also true that the Incarnation is an event which takes up all human acts and experiences into God's redemptive grace. Religion is not a "supernatural" element stretched above and separate from ordinary human reality. It is mistaken however to believe that values, beliefs and grace can be left nameless and implicit and that the lesson can still be called a religious one. The purpose of experience in the religious lesson is that it leads to or connects with explicitly religious understanding. This may be because it arouses wonder or puzzlement or a sense of moral responsibility. These can be, if well managed, experiences of disclosure out of which the explicit religious word of scripture or doctrinal teaching or liturgical celebration can arise without too much forcing. The now traditional method of See-Judge-Act is an earlier and still useful form of religious education through experience. Here, experience, the "facts of the week" were laid side by side with a passage from scripture. The hope was that the experience would be discussed in a way which would provoke some disclosure of its meaning, some questions of value.

Scripture would illuminate these and lead to action. Teaching through experience envisages a rather more subtle connection between experience and religious meaning. But the psychology of the process is the same.

184.   When we look at the use of experience in this way, we see that there must be some nodes, some turn, some crucial point at which the religious dimension begins: "the point of intersection of the timeless with time". This moment is indeed crucial and is very difficult to manage. There is a danger that it may be too contrived. Children begin with reflection on suffering or relationships, gifts or water. When they are confronted with the Passion of Christ or the Trinity, the Eucharist or Baptism, they may be left with a feeling that they have been led up the garden path. Some teachers, for this reason, shy away from the "point of intersection". There is no abstract answer to this difficulty. Success depends upon the teacher's sensitivity and ability. The vital importance of teacher-training, both initial and in-service is emphasised by this problem.

Thematic teaching

185. Thematic teaching is a style in which a lesson is built round a topic or an area of interest, rather than drawn from a disciplined form of knowledge such as a regular school subject. It draws in elements from various subjects. Its virtues when it is well done, are greater interest and better integrated learning, understanding and sensitivity. It is common to use this method in religious education; elements from geography, history, literature, science combining with explicit religious teaching (scriptural, doctrinal or liturgical) round a single theme which might be a tangible one like water or a more abstract one like friendship. It is a way of teaching religion which has much to recommend it. The principles which should be observed are that the specifically religious element should not be shirked; that the material should be well integrated in terms of a proper understanding of the relationship between natural and supernatural reality; that the links between "secular" and religious elements should be tested for both logical and psychological soundness.

The Integrated Curriculum

186. Many schools, especially primary schools, do not divide up the curriculum into subjects. Learning proceeds in a more informal way through topics and projects. In this case, religious education may find itself part of a broader curriculum. It may not have very much distinct existence as a classroom subject. Most of the principles which relate to themes apply here too. Although it may look informal and easy-going, a good integrated curriculum needs to be more carefully planned than a traditional differentiated one. This means that those who contribute to it must know what they are doing. Physics for infants as part of the integrated scheme, must be good physics. Equally, the religious element in an integrated curriculum must be proper religion. It must follow the principles for building up a religious curriculum which we have set out in this chapter. The danger is that it may become no more than vague religious feeling, just as the danger of the whole integrated curriculum when badly done, is that it will become confused and aimless.

Postscript on Morality

187. Some people think that christian morality should not be thought of as a separate content-area. Morality, they say, is a corollary, almost a part of faith. It is implicit in the liturgy. A major purpose of the use of life-experience in religious teaching is to enable Christians to see it in a moral light. Nevertheless modern life with its pluralism, its lack of a firm moral heritage and of social pressure has highlighted the importance of moral education. Moreover, although the ideal of christian morality may be St Augustine's "Love and do what you will", the Church has always found it necessary to express its moral teaching much more exactly and in much greater detail. This process of articulating the commandments of the new law into particular principles and rules goes back at least as far as St Paul. So there has grown up a body of moral teaching and we must say something about it.

188. There are two schools of thought about moral education at present. One we can characterise as: teach them what's right. The other as: teach them how to make up their minds. The first thinks of morality primarily in objective terms; in terms of visible and describable acts; objective principles and rules into which human behaviour must be fitted. It envisages a heritage of such principles and rules which are to a greater or less extent a part of christian revelation. Subjective factors — motive, intent, feeling, stress, relationship, circumstance — may lessen the degree of blame-worthiness. But the stuff of morality is what can be clearly formulated and placed in moral classes. For the other school of thought thoughtful personal decision is the essence of morality. Objective acts and the way they are judged remains an important factor. But intention and motive, circumstance and situation, the dynamics of personal choice stand in the foreground. Catholic teaching is that both these views contain some truth. If either goes its own way without the other, chaos will result. Catholic moral education must begin from a synthesis of them.

189. Let us begin with the first view. If we leave aside the moral teaching of the gospels and that embodied in the liturgy, it remains true that there is a vast body of Catholic moral teaching which has been issued. It goes right from the teaching of St Paul about meat offered to idols down to the teaching of Pope Paul VI on contraception and euthanasia. Of course the body of teaching has to be in some way taught and learned. There are a number of important points about how this should be done.

190. The first principle is that moral teaching, like doctrine, develops. The Church as it makes its way through history, guarding and expressing the word of God, constantly encounters new challenges and problems. It often takes quite a while to work out what are the right christian answers. This is especially true nowadays. For life is much more complex. Economics, sociology and psychology have developed rapidly. These human sciences offer us a great many facts and theories about the workings of human society and human nature. These facts are a necessary part of the judgements which the Church makes about moral issues. The Church teaches with unfailing authority in moral matters. But the exercise of that authority is not a simple black-and-white affair. So in learning Catholic moral teaching, it is not enough simply to say what it is. It is also necessary to learn how it develops in response to changing human circumstances, as well as in response to the word of God. As with doctrine, so with morals, a sense of development is needed; and this is not either doctrinal or moral relativism. Catholic doctrinal and moral teaching is unfailing. But it is never exhaustive. No human words about the things of God can ever be that.

191. Similarly, like the Church's doctrine, her moral teaching has an architecture and a shape. There is a hierarchy of principles and values as there is a hierarchy of truths. This also should emerge in moral teaching. It makes a difficult demand on teachers. It requires that they should understand the depth to which the Church is committed on any particular moral question; and that they should understand the basic principles and structure of Catholic teaching. This is not only necessary in justice and truthfulness. It is also pedagogically important. For we learn well when principles and structures are clear, badly when presented with a jumble of confused detail. This is a principle which highlights yet again, the importance of effective training of teachers and catechists.

192. When we speak of this "hierarchy of values" we must acknowledge that there is one overriding principle in christian morality which should inform all others. We refer to the primacy of love or charity which is the culmination and summary of our Lord's moral teaching in the gospels. Some people hold that love is not a moral principle but some kind of universal human force. We firmly teach that it is among other things, a moral principle and the first one, and that this truth must stand out plainly wherever christian morality is taught. We are not going to enter into endless arguments about the nature and justification of morality. But we must add that this means that christian morality in essence is to be thought of as a relationship. Laws and rules are necessary to show us how this relationship is to be worked out in our lives. Laws and rules are dangerous if they become so many and so detailed that the primacy of charity is lost sight of. This was the case of the Pharisees to whom, of all the people he met, our Lord showed the strongest moral disapproval. To sum this question up: it is necessary to know the Church's moral teaching; it is necessary to know its shape and have a sound awareness of the strength of authority which each particular teaching has; and it is necessary to see and feel how each principle is a way of expressing our love of God. We might sum it up still more pithily by saying that a Catholic is one who is aware of belonging to a community of moral wisdom and who lives as a member of it.

193. We now turn to the other school of thought which is that the purpose of moral education is to enable people to make up their own minds about moral questions. This is a popular view (cf. the work of John Wilson in the Farmington Trust, and Peter McPhail in the "Lifeline" project). Its premise is that we live in a morally pluralistic age. There is no generally accepted set of moral principles and rules. For that situation, moral education has to enable young people to find their own way in moral matters, to achieve moral autonomy. The idea is to filter off substantial moral principles and values, and concentrate on those abilities which make possible a personal moral act. Then a young person, Christian or not, can set off properly equipped through the jungle of diverse moral ideologies.

194. The weakness of this view is obvious enough. The idea of freewheeling moral abilities working without any definite moral values is rather like a mill-wheel grinding away on itself without any grain to get hold of. The only result is the machinery gets damaged or that the mill gets closed down because it is futile. What results sometimes is a state of moral scepticism, even cynicism. However, it is true that choosing and deciding in moral matters, especially in the modern world where things are not absolutely clear, does not just come naturally to us. It is something to be learned. Indeed it requires a number of different abilities which we have to learn. Knowledge is required for moral decision. If I am weighing up whether to tell the whole truth to a gravely ill person for instance, I need to know the facts of the case. Again we have to be able to predict the probable outcome

II

of our actions; what is likely to happen for instance if I drive a car very fast on a busy greasy road. We need to have some insight into our own feelings and an awareness of the feelings of others. We have to be able to understand a moral principle and to apply it to concrete cases. None of these are innate abilities. All of them are necessary for making responsible moral decisions.

195. We find further support for this view in the morality of the New Testament. Goodness, our Lord teaches, does not only consist of external acts. It is a matter also of motive and intent. It comes from the heart. "It is what comes out of a man that makes him unclean. For it is from within men's hearts that evil intentions emerge: fornication, theft, murder, adultery, avarice, malice, deceit, indecency, envy, slander, pride, folly. All these evil things come from within and make a man unclean" (Mk 7:20-23). So the dynamics of personal decision — the moral education of the mind and heart — also has a valid claim on us.

196. So in the moral aspect of religious education, we need to integrate the idea of learning a body of moral teaching with the idea of learning how to make moral decisions properly. As in the case of doctrine, the unifying factor is the idea of tradition. To initiate young people into a tradition means that they come to share its faith and moral values. They become aware of belonging to a community of moral wisdom which has a distinctive teaching and a definite authority. But that community is alive and growing. It is not a finally completed thing and it does not dictate the whole of our lives absolutely. Therefore, within it, there is the need for personal responsibility and a measure of moral autonomy.

Content and Method

197. We have written at length about content. What methods are best in catechesis is a much more open question. For here, psychological and pedagogical considerations are of great importance. Moreover, personal factors — a teacher's style, the mentality and outlook of a class — are also important. Still, it is true that when we reflect on the content of catechesis, some approaches to method arise out of that. So, the principle of *function* — what do we hope that the use of scriptural or doctrinal or liturgical material, will *achieve* — already dictates to some extent, how that material should be handled.

198. Nonetheless, a number of other factors are of great importance. Methods must not only make for good learning theoretically. They must also create motivation and interest. They must encourage involvement. They must take into account age, ability and social background. They will be different for children and for adults. They will vary with the setting — classroom, discussion group, residential course, liturgical catechesis. They will include straightforward instruction. But there is also room for discussion and discovery methods. These may well be more successful in promoting personal faith. There is also a place for activity — mime, drama, the visual arts. While other methods may touch the mind more directly, these may well touch effectively, the more remote and difficult areas of attitude and feeling.

Chapter 8

The Way Ahead

Conclusion — Aims, Policies and Practice

200. It is clear from the previous chapters that catechesis is not a simple process. To establish it on a sound foundation we must give due weight to theological principles. But we must also do justice to the patterns of individual growth and to the character and formative power of our present society. In this final chapter we will try to draw these threads together. In the first part we will set out the nature, types and aims of catechesis. In the second we will describe how our Church community in England and Wales should carry out its catechetical task.

PART 1

The Nature of Catechesis

201. Catechesis is that form of the ministry of the word which leads faith towards maturity. Two things should be noted about this definition. First, catechesis assumes some degree of shared faith. The one who is catechised must have a personal faith, at least the potential faith which is the gift of Baptism and at least some connection with the Church community. So, catechesis is distinct from evangelisation which does not assume faith. It aims at conversion or re-conversion — including that daily re-conversion to God in faith which is required of all of us. Evangelisation as well as catechesis is necessary even within the Church community, in parish and school. But here our concern is with catechesis.

Secondly, in using the phrase "maturity of faith" we are recalling what was said in Chapter 3. Briefly, mature faith is personal, thoughtful and active. It is not solely in the mind but is closer to a relationship or an attitude. It permeates the whole of a believer's life and gives it direction. It enables him to understand the meaning of his experience, of events and of the world he lives in.

The Goals of Catechesis

202. The overall aim of catechesis is expressed in its definition. We are using the word "goals" to describe its more specific aims. By way of expanding the definition we add only one thing. All catechesis should be centred on Christ. All the elements in a mature faith must relate to the relationship we make in him, with the Father, through the working of the Holy Spirit. It is true that we cannot deduce everything that must be done from that principle. But it must be the framework within which all our analysis of the goals must exist. These goals are:

(a) To develop a knowledge and understanding of the holy scriptures and a sensitivity to them as the word of God speaking in our lives.

(b) To develop a knowledge of Catholic doctrine understood in the light of its development in tradition under the teaching authority of the Church.

(c) To develop an ability to pray which can grow and deepen.

(d) To develop an ability to understand and to share actively and personally in the liturgy.

(e) To promote a sense of belonging to the Church which will lead to an active participation in its life.

(f) To promote a faith which gives unity and meaning to personal life, to responsibilities and events which occur.

(g) To promote the ability to relate to others in a way that reflects the evangelical commandment of love.

(h) To develop the ability to make moral judgements and decisions and to see them as a way of realising a relationship with Christ.

(i) To promote the ability to discern christian values in life in this world and to act in accordance with them.

Types of Catechesis

203. The norm for all catechesis is the *Catechumenate* in which adult converts are prepared for Baptism. This principle was set out by *The General Catechetical Directory* and emphasised by the Synod of 1977. It is the model which all other kinds of catechesis should imitate. So, it is not denied that there are other kinds of catechesis. But they must look to adult catechesis and try to adapt its main characteristics to their own subjects and settings. It is true that the adult catechumenate is not common. But it was universal in the early centuries of the Church and in recent years it has been revived in some countries. We must try to describe its main characteristics.

204.

(a) The first of these is that this catechesis is an *initiation.* It is true that an adult who asks for Baptism already has some faith and some connection with the Church. The purpose of catechesis is to bring him to full faith and full membership. This goes beyond the learning of scripture or doctrine, beyond learning how to join in liturgical ceremonies. Its basic idea is *bringing inside.* Its function is to bring new members inside the faith, as outlook of mind, as community, as moral way of life. The specific elements of this catechesis are only means to that end. There are three principal means. First there is instruction, explanation of scripture, of doctrine and of christian life. The high point of this is the handing over of the Creed, the classical expression of the faith which the new convert inherits. Secondly there are the new and growing relationships which catechesis involves: between the converts and their sponsors, their catechists and the whole Church community. Thirdly the initiation is accomplished by ritual symbol and ceremony, the laying on of hands, anointing, the lighted candle.

(b) The second characteristic is that this catechesis is one of climax or event. It is progressive, it leads on through various stages to the Easter Vigil and the sacraments of initiation. The catechesis is built round this climactic event and builds up to it.

(c) Thirdly and consequently, this catechesis has a strong liturgical colouring. Much of the day-to-day work will consist of instruction or discussion. But the whole process has a liturgical context. Liturgy marks out its stages, and forms, we might say, its curriculum. Liturgy, as we have said in an earlier chapter, has its own distinctive catechetical, educational power.

(d) Finally, the catechumenate is for adults. Therefore it depends upon an act of adult choice; upon at least some degree of deliberation, reflection and free option. Its climax (Baptism) is received after an act of informed and thoughtful choice. *The General Catechetical Directory* describes the aims of catechesis as to promote "free adherence to God in faith". Only adults are really capable of such faith. That is why the *Directory* takes the adult catechumenate as the ideal towards which all catechesis should look. It is true that the adult catechumenate, in the strict sense, scarcely exists in this country. But there are some places where it could be revived and we strongly urge that this should be done. A fresh start would be especially timely in view of the new rite of the *Christian Initiation of Adults*. If it can be realised even in a few parishes, we will have among us, a living example, rather than an abstract model.

The Catechesis of Children

205. We go on now to consider some of the most important of the other forms of catechesis. The first is the catechesis of children. In our Church community, the effect of the primacy of the adult catechumenate can be seen in the recent and rapid development of religious education for adults. Yet most of our resources, both financial and human, are still spent on catechising children. This is a process which has its own distinctive character and its own special problems. The chief of these is: How can the catechesis of children model itself on the adult catechumenate? The difficulty arises from the fourth characteristic of adult catechesis. For children do not have the maturity or the experience to make this reflective, "free adherence to God in faith". This has led some people to speak of the religious teaching given to children as a "pre-catechesis", and to regard children themselves as in some way "pre-Christians". There is a serious confusion here which needs to be cleared up.

(a) It is true that the catechesis given to children (as a school subject or otherwise) should look towards adult faith. This means that it must not allow people to get stuck at infantile expressions and ideas of their faith. It must build round the central truths of the faith. These can grow and expand indefinitely. Marginal things (whether doctrinal or devotional) have on the other hand, no capacity for growth. Too much emphasis on them (or the wrong kind of emphasis) can lead to a permanently infantile faith. Children should take an active part in catechesis (for example, through activity methods, making up their own prayers, etc.) In this way, a growing faith will become part of their general growth. Catechists should encourage questions and discussion. They must expect criticism, sometimes rejection. Adult faith develops through rethinking and through crises. It cannot be achieved painlessly.

(b) The catechesis of children should lead to adult faith. Their religious life is limited in many ways; especially in its ideas and in its degree of freedom. But it is not a mere preparatory stage. Faith is not the same as a process of human growth and fulfilment. Children who are baptised are true Christians and full members of the Church. Moreover, the religion of childhood has its own positive value. Children often have a simplicity of heart and a sense of wonder which adults have lost. While having an eye on the development of faith, catechists should nourish these qualities. It is no part of our business to destroy them in the interests of an intellectual and more sophisticated religion.

Catechesis of Events

206. There are certain key points in life when there are special possibilities for catechesis; and also a special need for it. Some of them are strictly religious. Others are just the great landmarks of human life itself. They include the first approach to the Holy Eucharist and the sacrament of Penance, growing up, the choice of a vocation, marriage, sickness and death. Most of them are in some way connected with a sacrament. Especially nowadays, we have come to see the sacraments as centres of a network of pastoral care and catechetical work. This is emphasised in the new rites for the sacrament of Penance and for the anointing and pastoral care of the sick. Sometimes this catechesis will take place in the parish; sometimes in the home; sometimes in the school. Sometimes, as in the case of first Communion, all these will combine. Sometimes other agencies will play a part. For example, the courses offered by the Catholic Marriage Advisory Council are catechesis of this kind. It is important that all the catechetical possibilities in the situation be exploited. There is a chance for doctrinal learning (for instance about the nature of the sacrament and its place in christian life). There is also an opportunity for the education of feeling and attitude (for instance through liturgy). Moral education has a place too, especially in preparation for the sacrament of Penance through which a true and mature christian moral outlook should emerge. The strength of this kind of catechesis is that all these different aspects can be unified in the same event or sacrament.

207.   Many people equate catechesis with instruction. In recent centuries "learning your catechism" has been its commonest form. Nowadays, it is not so highly valued nor so widely practised. Yet it still has an irreplaceable worth. Instruction takes as its materials, those expressions of faith which come to us in the form of knowledge. It limits itself to cognitive learning and this is the most straightforward and the best understood kind. Religious instruction should not be blind. It should aim at understanding. Indeed, much of what we have said in Chapter 7 about the learning of doctrine, applies here. It should aim at comprehensibility, coherence, a sense of development and relevance. But it is not the only kind. Knowledge about and understanding of the holy scriptures and Church history also have catechetical value. Instruction seems rather pedestrian. It is sometimes dismissed as "mere knowledge". Yet, like other forms of catechesis it does mature faith. It gives it a more secure basis. It strengthens faith in time of doubt and trial. It satisfies our need to understand. It helps us to see the consequences of faith for our own lives. Instructional catechesis need not be kept in a separate compartment, indeed it should be effectively integrated with other forms. But it remains an indispensable element.

The Liturgical Type

208.   Liturgy is involved in several of the types of catechesis already mentioned: initiatory catechesis and the catechesis of event. But there is also a regular element of catechesis in the whole of the liturgy, as it is celebrated throughout the year and throughout our lives. We repeat what was said in Chapter 7. Liturgy is not *for* catechesis. It is for God. Still, though that is its essence, catechesis and formation should be among its effects. Liturgical catechesis does transmit knowledge: for instance through the hearing of God's word and explanation of and reflection on it. Yet, as we have said, its main effect is in shaping our feelings and attitudes. It has a special power since it does this through our relationship with God in the christian community.

We can extend the idea of liturgical catechesis beyond the official liturgy of the Church. There is a legitimate paraliturgy; events constructed in a way similar to the liturgy, but usually with a more direct catechetical purpose. These express a theme of the faith through music, poetry, mime, dance and drama. As a form of catechesis they have two strengths. The first is that those who take part are active and so find the theme more memorable.

Secondly it is a kind of catechesis useful for (and very acceptable to) those who are mentally handicapped or not very intelligent, and for whom instructional catechesis would not be effective.

The Educational Type

209. All of these types of catechesis overlap and mingle together. The distinctions are not made on the same criteria. Nonetheless they are worth describing separately for each of them has some distinctive features which are important both in theory and in practice. By "the educational type" we mean that mode of catechesis which takes place in the setting of formal education. This means that usually (though not always) it will take place in school. Educational catechesis must work within the limits of the classroom, of compulsory attendance, of curriculum and timetable. It also means that it must abide by the ideas of education which are generally established. In this country at present it is generally believed that to "count" as education, a subject must pass several tests. It must involve an initiation into some worthwhile area of thought or of experience. It must be set in a rational tradition. It must promote or at least have room for "autonomy", that is the ability of young people to stand on their own feet and make their own choices. It is sometimes argued that only a neutral or "non-confessional" religious education can meet these standards. We do not think so. We believe that Christianity studied in a spirit of faith can be educational in this sense; at least if the standards are not applied too dogmatically. Of course we agree that educational catechesis (like any other kind) must avoid indoctrination: when that word is understood to mean manipulating children's feelings, or attempting to close their minds against criticism or against future growth.

Educational catechesis is bound to give a high priority to reason and understanding. It has, therefore, a close connection with instructional catechesis as we described that earlier. But the classroom nowadays, is not only a place for instruction. There is a new interest in the education of emotions and attitudes. Catechesis in school is often a catechesis of event: for example schools are often given the lion's share in preparing children for first Communion, Confession, or Confirmation. But the schools should not be expected to bear the whole responsibility for this. They should work in close collaboration with parents and with parishes. It is exactly in this close connection between the school and the local Church community that the strength of our English Dual System consists. There is also the possibility of a liturgical catechesis, in the preparation and celebration of classroom Masses and in the work connected with the liturgical seasons of the year. Moreover the classroom is not the school. The school has a larger community life. This is expressed in its worship, but also through pastoral care through the quality of relationships. Through these also, another range of catechetical possibilities is opened up.

Catechesis given in the classroom remains a very important form. It is the one into which we have put most of our resources. Yet classroom teaching inevitably involves limitations. Inevitably it narrows the possible range of catechetical experiences. So we should not expect miracles from classroom teaching. We should have realistic and limited expectations of it. We have always agreed that schools can do little without the support of the home. We must take this fact more effectively into account in our practice. If teachers are indiscriminately loaded with all the catechetical responsibilities of the Church, they will easily become discouraged. It would be indeed far too heavy a responsibility. If the Church community sets them more limited and reasonable goals, teachers will take courage and set out to achieve these. Beyond that, the Church community must mobilise itself to meet the rest of our catechetical responsibilities. In the next and last Section we will see how this is to be done.

PART 2

The Church Community and Catechesis

210. "Catechesis is the task of the whole Church community". In these words or others, this principle is stated by *The General Catechetical Directory* and repeated by the Synod of 1977. What has been said so far in *Cornerstone* should reinforce this principle. Catechesis has not one but a number of aims. It occurs not in one but in a number of settings. It involves not only one group of professional educators but almost every group of people within the Church. We must try now to see how this principle of advancing not on one but on several fronts can be realised. First it is not a principle which discounts or undervalues the work of professionals — clergy, teachers, catechists of all kinds. They are needed not only for the direct task of catechesis. They are also needed to help and support the others who are not professionals but who have a catechetical responsibility. It is clear that a large number of these latter must undertake some form of catechesis. To enable them to do this, a serious and large-scale effort in adult education is needed.

211. The basis and the importance of adult education have been emphasised several times in this book. Programmes of adult education already exist in many parts of the country. So, we are not proposing anything new; merely drawing threads together and summarising. The first reason for adult education is simply that faith, ideally, is an adult act. It is, under grace, a free informed and thoughtful choice. Therefore, however strong it may have been in childhood, faith must re-establish itself in adult life at its own proper level. This is especially true and especially obvious in the modern world. For it is a world which does not offer faith much support. Faith has to be well-founded and able to stand on its own two feet. In the Church too, the expressions of the faith are changing. So too is liturgical practice and the general atmosphere. Those who are full and active members of the Church must learn to live with change while preserving an undisturbed faith and a loyalty to Catholic tradition. For all these reasons, continuous catechesis is an urgent necessity.

Also, in our times we have seen a broadening of the idea of ministry. Catechesis is not an ordained ministry like say, the diaconate. But it is an official service in the church. All who catechise share in that. Hence the second reason for developing adult education. It is a preparation for that ministry. Put it in those terms, and you see immediately why it cannot be a purely intellectual affair. It would be better to speak of Adult Catechesis than Adult Education. It is the preparation of parents and others for their catechetical task. This not only requires knowledge of the scriptures, of doctrine and liturgy. It also depends on the quality of the catechist's own faith.

Hence we urge the development of adult catechesis in our Church community through all the agencies which are able to undertake it. We urge all Catholics to support it. We have already pointed out the risk this runs; the danger that the faith may become too intellectual, restricted to a small, sophisticated group. We must take care that this does not happen. We must make sure that the little ones, the "poor of Jahwe" receive the catechesis they need. But this risk should not deter us from the development of adult catechists. Indeed one of its functions should be to support parents and those responsible for the mentally handicapped and the underprivileged in their catechetical work.

The Diocese

212. The bishop, we believe, is the chief catechist. This follows from his role as a successor of the apostles and chief pastor of a local Church. Our principle of church government is that each diocese is independent under the supreme authority of the Holy See. The policy in recent years has been to leave dioceses more freedom of action so that they can respond more positively to local situations and needs. Often there are problems which are common to all the dioceses in a particular country. Hence national Bishops' Conferences also have the power to decide some issues and to form some policies. National governments now control more and more of life, and the mass media more effectively form common attitudes in each country. Hence these national policies have come to assume nowadays, a greater importance.

The bishop, the chief pastor, cannot do everything himself. Nonetheless he does have a direct catechetical task. This he exercises as he goes about the diocese, visiting, preaching, confirming, ordaining, and also in his pastoral letters. He has also another catechetical function, less direct but much more widespread. This is the task of making sure that the various catechetical agencies in a diocese — family, parish and school — are working well. He must ensure that they have sufficient help and support and even more important, that they are working well together. Few things are more destructive than to have different agencies at cross purposes with each other — parish against school, school against family. The bishop must co-ordinate these various agencies, gathering them together within a single catechetical policy. In this he needs the help of a diocesan catechetical team.

The Diocesan Team

213. The diocesan catechetical team has a universal role which cannot be defined abstractly. Dioceses vary. Some have a dense population, small in area and with many schools. In some ways this is an advantage. There is plenty of "plant". But in another way it can be a disadvantage. For often it brings with it a large number of urban problems; the social and religious problems associated with the inner city and with new towns. The diocesan team must assess the needs of the diocese and work to respond to these. It must balance the various demands; help for schools, work in parish catechesis, adult education, work with families, the training of catechists, the production of teaching materials. There is no abstract blue-print for success. This will depend on a well-informed realistic assessment of the situation and an intelligent pastoral decision about where the available resources can be used best. Diocesan teams must be in regular contact with all the catechetical agencies in the diocese: schools and parishes, the clergy, teacher and parent organisations, groups which care for the handicapped. A council which includes representatives of the diocesan team along with those of other involved bodies may be useful. It might unify the concerns of parishes and clergy, parents, school administrators and catechists. It might forestall conflicts and promote an integrated catechetical policy.

The Parish

214. The parish is concerned with general pastoral care. But catechetical work of one kind or another is a major element in this. The catechetical work of the parish falls mainly under three heads.

(a) *Liturgical Catechesis*

The parish is formed and held together by the regular celebration of the liturgy of the Church. Clergy and laity should be involved in the preparation of this liturgy. We have said already (see Chapter 7) that liturgy is not catechesis. But the connection is a close one. All those involved should be aware of the catechetical dimension of liturgy, and should work to realise this in the parish. Homilies should be prepared with the principles of liturgical catechesis in mind. So far as possible the other aspects of parochial catechesis (for instance the parish school, catechetical classes and family groups) should try to chime in with the parish celebration of the liturgy.

(b) *Catechesis of Event*

The parish is also the setting within which most of the major events of christian and human life are celebrated and consecrated; birth, growing-up, marriage, death. Each of these events forms the centre of a catechesis. The catechesis of events is of great importance because it is connected with occasions which mean so much to us and which shape our lives. Pastors and all concerned must make sure that the catechesis connected with these events is effective. It should be well thought-out. It should also be of a piece with the general pastoral work of the parish.

(c) *Formal Catechesis*

The two aspects of catechesis just mentioned are embedded in the general life and work of the parish. But it also has catechetical tasks of a more explicit and formal kind. In some places, there is no parish school, and the whole work of the catechesis of children has to be done in some other setting. In others there are many children not in Church schools and these have to be

126

looked after. Again, some parishes believe that the catechesis offered by the school, while admirable, is not sufficient. It needs to be complemented by catechesis of some other kind. So, even so far as children are concerned, a parish may be faced with considerable catechetical responsibilities. In the case of adult education, the task is even greater. The parish should be the main centre round which adults build their christian lives. All parishes should offer some form of adult catechesis. In today's world, parishes must face up, really seriously to this task. Where there is a parish council it must make this one of its first priorities. Many parishes need to consider the possibility of appointing (and paying) a full-time catechist. This would not be someone on to whom all the work could be off-loaded. It would be someone whose main task would be to co-ordinate and support the work of voluntary catechesis and parents working in the parish.

The Deanery

215. Some forms of catechesis need to be organised on a wider basis than that of the parish. This is especially true of adult education where professional speakers and teachers have to be found. In some areas (especially in the cities) the deanery offers a very suitable setting for this. It is large enough to have considerable resources. It is small enough for everyone to know each other and for the social situation to be more or less the same. We strongly recommend that Deanery Conferences consider very seriously what catechetical initiatives they could take. In many places we believe, they could be the main agencies for the catechesis of adults; and of support for parents and others whose catechetical work is of an informed and non-professional kind.

The School

216. Our schools have served the Catholic community well. We stand greatly in the debt of those who established and maintained them and of those who have taught in them. The school, like the Church by and large, must be flexible and adaptable enough to meet new times and new challenges. Schools now have to educate children in a very different social climate from that our grandparents knew. The schools themselves have been drawn much more efficiently into our national education system. They are strongly influenced by the ideas and trends which are found in the general world of education. A couple of generations ago their relations with that world were very cautious. They were rooted mainly in Church life. In many ways this change has been all to the good. We have looked at the theological basis for it in Chapter 5. But it does sometimes create problems about the distinctive identity of our Church schools and their distinctive contribution.

Our teaching in this book has been that catechesis is a spectrum of different styles and modes. It should involve the whole of the Church community. Each section of that community should have a clear idea of what is expected of it. Perhaps in the past we have had excessive expectations of our schools. We have left almost every aspect of catechesis to them. So we must try to say now what tasks our schools can realistically be expected to do. We will put this in terms of a minimum and maximum; expectations and hopes, requirements and ideals.

Religious Education

217. One basic duty of a Catholic school, is to provide religious education in the classroom. This must be of at least as good a professional standard as any other subject. Catholic schools have a serious duty to meet its needs. It must have a fair allocation of staff and of posts of responsibility. It must have a fair share in the requisition of teaching materials. The training of religious education teachers both initial and in-service, must be an important priority over the next few years. In Chapters 5 and 7 and earlier in this chapter, we have given an account of what the character of this subject should be: of its aims and its content in the classroom. Catholic schools are concerned with the educational form of catechesis.

The School Community

218. The Vatican document on *The Catholic School* (1977) lays great stress on the importance of the school as a christian community. Indeed if the school is not to some extent, a community of faith, classroom religion is likely to become little more than an academic exercise. If it is, then the formal catechesis has somewhere to put its roots. Building and maintaining the school as a christian community is a task that has to be constantly worked at. We wish to emphasise these important aspects of it.

The first is worship. A Catholic school should have a liturgy which lives and speaks. As many people as possible should prepare and participate in it. An effective community liturgy depends of course on the community already existing. But it also helps to create and sustain it.

Secondly, a Catholic school should consciously try to organise

128

its life in the light of the values and beliefs on which it is established. Many aspects of that life — for instance, discipline and attitudes to work, pastoral care, extra curricular activities, even school meals, can reflect the gospel or fail to do so.

Thirdly, the building of a christian community depends on being at least a large nucleus of committed teachers who are prepared to work at the task. We must ensure the supply of Catholic teachers of this quality and support them with in-service training and with whatever other kind of help is needed. Many christian teachers of other denominations can fit very well into the community of our schools and do valuable work there. In building the school into a christian community, the head teacher and the school chaplain are both key figures.

The School as Missionary

219. The school is never going to be a perfect christian community any more than the whole Church is. The school is a chip off the old block. We should not be surprised if it contains its due proportion of sinners, mere conformists, the disinterested, the doubtful, the disbelieving. Both in its formal religious teaching and through the quality of its community life, the school should make allowance for these "degrees of belonging". We do not have to be evangelistic or revivalist to fulfil a mission. The mission of the school is shaped by what a school is capable of. It can and it should, both in the religious lessons and in school life, offer something of real religious value even to those whose faith is scarcely discernible.

The school also has a mission to the local community. Parental involvement in schools has recently increased greatly. Catholic schools especially should try to draw parents into their pastoral and catechetical tasks. In this way they will promote better co-ordination and the sense of a shared enterprise. They may be able to go beyond that. Some schools already offer to parents and to others in the Church community, courses and meetings, religious education at their own level, designed to deepen and inform their own faith. We strongly urge that ventures of this kind be multiplied. They are foremost among the ideals and hopes we have for our schools.

The School and the local Church

220. The last point leads us on to consider the place of schools in the local Church. Sometimes it is a source of conflict. A school which is labelled "progressive" is at odds with a local

I

Church dominated by traditional attitudes. Sometimes the opposite happens. The governors, heads and staffs of schools and the pastors of the local Churches must make conscious and positive effort to overcome these conflicts and to replace them by co-operation. For the school and the local Church have a lot to give to each other. Better relations with parents, more regular contacts with local clergy are two of the ways in which this can be done. Another is in what we have called the "catechesis of event", especially in the preparation for the sacraments. Programmes of preparation for first Communion or for Confirmation can be planned which involve family, parish and school. These reduce conflict, promote mutual understanding and form a most valuable and helpful catechesis for the children themselves.

Teachers and Catechists

221. Teachers think of themselves primarily as professionals; equipped with the skills to do a highly professional job. The word catechist on the other hand, has the force rather of a ministry in the Church. This account of the expectations and hopes we have for Church Schools, seems to imply that all those who work in them should see themselves as involved at least indirectly in a catechetical ministry. Not all Catholic teachers are willing to accept that idea. But there must be a substantial nucleus of teachers who have a deep sense of their vocation as well as a professional approach to their career. These teacher/catechists are key figures, usually outside school as well as in it. They need and deserve support and help in their professional and catechetical work. They also need spiritual formation and guidance. To provide this is an important part of the responsibility of the school chaplain.

Other Groups

222. The Synod of 1977 laid great stress on the idea of "basic communities". These are small groups whose closely shared life is based on shared faith. The Synod recommended these as ideal settings for catechesis. For they offer the experience of a faith lived in common, as well as the chance to learn the expressions of that faith. Many groups of this sort are springing up in various parts of the world. It is true that they tend to flourish where other settings for catechesis are not available. Nevertheless the idea is an important one. In England and Wales many small groups have grown up in the last few years: family groups, study groups, prayer groups. They represent a considerable potential for catechesis of both adults and children. We hope over the next few years to develop a more systematic approach to catechesis through these small groups.

There are other groups which organise youth days, catechetical camps and other residential courses. They all work on the principle of offering a different and concentrated experience of the faith; living and praying it together for a few days, as well as discussing its content and problems. They represent an important line of development for the future. The formulations of the faith are relatively simple to transmit but easily go abstract and dead. The experience of faith always has life in it but is very hard to transmit. We need to explore ways such as these in which the emphasis is on experience.

Special Situations

223. Every member of the Church has the right to receive appropriate catechesis. For a considerable number, the ordinary ways are inadequate. This is usually because they suffer from some handicap. They may be deaf, blind or mentally handicapped. They have a special call on us. This is, that the Church is not about human fulfilment, maturity or normality. The gospel teaches us that failure, while not to be sought out, has a positive value.

We insist that the handicapped are not saved by some extra-ordinary grace. They are full members of the Church. They and their families have the right to all the helps they need to enable them to share in its life. So they need not only physical and emotional support, but also a true catechesis. Clearly in many cases, this catechesis needs to be drastically adapted. This again has a positive value. It teaches us something about catechesis when it has to be offered to those who cannot form concepts and can hardly express themselves in words.

We urge that full support be given to those who are doing this demanding work. Catechesis for the deaf is already well developed in many parts of the country. We are glad to see that in recent years, catechesis of the mentally handicapped is being tackled with a new seriousness. A National Advisory Council for Special Religious Education now exists to co-ordinate all this work: to sort out the problems in it; to offer training and prepare materials. We hope that its work will grow and be fruitful; that this area of catechesis will not be a neglected one but will receive special emphasis and privilege.

The National Dimension

224. There are some tasks in catechesis which need to be tackled nationally; some because they are beyond the scope and resources of dioceses and local centres; some simply because they are national problems. The main tasks are these:

(a) The development and expression of an idea of catechesis which is true to the Church's present understanding of herself and to the needs of our changing society. The need for this will continue as times change and new problems occur.

(b) The development of research in religious education. This will include identifying the problems which need research; finding bodies which will undertake and support these projects; making available the results of research in other fields.

(c) Creating and maintaining links with international catechetical bodies especially in Europe and in the English-speaking world. The purpose of this that the Church in this country may benefit from what is thought and done elsewhere. Also our Church should offer the fruits of its own experience to others.

(d) To create and develop ecumenical links in religious education. There is a considerable amount of common ground between the Churches. There is the prospect of further joint projects of various kinds.

(e) To serve as a clearing-house for ideas in catechesis; and a focal point for the problems which local bodies find in their work; to prevent unnecessary overlap and promote co-ordination.

(f) To be a source of information about catechetical problems, and of teaching materials for catechesis at all levels.

"By the little rivers", wrote St Thomas Aquinas, "strive to come to the sea". The realisation of God's kingdom is not brought about by one dramatic event. It comes through many small channels. Our policy in catechesis must be to make sure that all of these channels are working and are kept clear.

"For while the tired waves vainly breaking,
Seem here no painful inch to gain,
Far back, through creeks and inlets making,
Comes silent, flooding in, the main."

INDEX

133

135